The Saints' Guide to
JOY THAT NEVER FADES

The Saints' Guide to
JOY THAT NEVER FADES

Ann Ball

CHARIS

SERVANT PUBLICATIONS
ANN ARBOR, MICHIGAN

Charis Books is an imprint of Servant Publications especially designed to serve
Roman Catholics.

Published by Servant Publications
P.O. Box 8617
Ann Arbor, Michigan 48107

Cover design by Paul Higdon, Minneapolis, Minn.

01 02 03 10 9 8 7 6 5 4 3 2 1

Printed in the United States of America
ISBN 0-56955-263-0

Library of Congress Cataloging-in-Publication Data

Ball, Ann.
The saints' guide to joy that never fades / Ann Ball.
    p. cm.
Includes bibliographical references and index.
ISBN 1-56955-263-0 (alk. paper)
  1. Christian saints. 2. Joy--Religious aspects--Christianity. I. Title.

BX4655.2 .B27 2001
282'.092'2--dc21
                                                              2001002919

DEDICATION

All of the glamorous advertisements and proud achieve-
ments in this life can't begin to compare to the joys of life-
everlasting union with the God of perfect beauty and
majesty. The good things in this life are simply a dress
rehearsal for the next, and death is the curtain call.

Ronda de Sola Chervin

This book is lovingly dedicated to my friend Judy Burns, who
consoled us as we wished to console her and who kept us
laughing.

Once at a meeting at my house, we were all seated around a
table when Judy got a funny look on her face. Because Judy was
frightened of cats, I usually threw my felines out of the house
when she came to visit. However, this time one had eluded me
and jumped into Judy's lap.

Horrified, I offered to remove the offender. Judy courageously responded, "No. I never touched a cat before. Can I
pet it?" When I assured her that she could, she touched its
soft fur. Overcoming her fear, she found the experience not
unpleasant.

That Christmas I received a card from Judy. The front depicted
a woman surrounded by cats. It read, "Merry Christmas to
you ..." Inside it continued, "and to your d—— cats, too!"

Judy, this book is for you! You touched a cat, you touched
my heart, now touch our God in joy and happiness forever.

CONTENTS

INTRODUCTION

What Is Joy, and Why Should We Have It?

The word *joy* comes from the same Latin word as *rejoicing*; it connotes great happiness. As one of the twelve fruits of the Holy Spirit, joy is the pleasure experienced by one who knows Christ as the ultimate happiness.

> The *fruits* of the Spirit are perfections that the Holy Spirit forms in us as the first fruits of eternal glory. The tradition of the Church lists twelve of them: "charity, joy, peace, patience, kindness, goodness, generosity, gentleness, faithfulness, modesty, self-control, chastity."[1]
>
> *Catechism of the Catholic Church*

The *Catechism* reminds us that our joy will be most intense and even perfect in heaven.

> In the glory of heaven the blessed continue joyfully to fulfill God's will in relation to other men and to all creation. Already they reign with Christ; with him "they shall reign for ever and ever."[2]

The psalmist commands us: "Shout joyfully to the Lord, all you lands; worship the Lord with cries of gladness; come before him with joyful song" (Ps 100:1-2). He reminds us, "Let the faithful [saints] rejoice in their glory, cry out for joy at their banquet" (Ps 149:5).

Christianity is a joyful religion. The beloved disciple John gives us the promise of Christ, "I have told you this so that my joy might be in you and your joy might be complete" (Jn 15:11).

Dorothy Day, in telling the story of her conversion, said, "Objectors cannot say that it was fear of loneliness and solitude and pain that made me turn to Him. It was in those few years when I was alone and most happy that I found Him; I found Him at last through joy and thanksgiving, not through sorrow. Yet, how can I say that either? Better let it be said that I found Him in His poor, and in a moment of joy I turned to Him."[3]

It was the birth of her child that led Day to faith. In *The Long Loneliness* she wrote, "No human creature could receive or contain so vast a flood of love and joy as I often felt after the birth of my child; with this came the need to worship, to adore." She decided to have Tamar Teresa baptized, and that led her to come into the Church herself.[4]

The saints knew and revered holy joy. Along sometimes rocky and tumultuous paths, they used humor to lighten the load. Sometimes even at the point of death they were able to show this animation and to impress their tormentors with the strength their joyful faith called forth. Their joy in the face of all obstacles is living proof of the promise of the Lord that our sorrow will be turned into laughter:

So you also are now in anguish. But I will see you again, and your hearts will rejoice, and no one will take your joy away from you.

JOHN 16:22

Blessed Abbot Marmion tells us that "joy is the echo of God's life in us!" Yet Christians in today's world are often stressed out, sad, and grieving. The example of faithful yet very human saints can bring us closer to Him who is all joy. Let us learn from them, that this echo might reverberate in our lives.

ONE

The Kingdom of Eternal Bliss

For this reason they stand before God's throne and worship him day and night in his temple. The one who sits on the throne will shelter them. They will not hunger or thirst anymore, nor will the sun or any heat strike them. For the Lamb who is in the center of the throne will shepherd them and lead them to springs of life-giving water, and God will wipe away every tear from their eyes.

REVELATION 7:15-17

St. Aelred was an English abbot, homilist, and historian. He became the superior of all the Cistercians in England and was instrumental in converting the warlike Picts. Eloquent in his sermons, he gained the title "the Bernard of England" because his writings reflect the theological soundness and beauty of style of St. Bernard of Clairvaux.

About the year 1160, St. Aelred wrote to his sister about heaven:

Let the glorious procession go into the high Jerusalem, the everlasting city of heaven. Christ Himself will be at its head, and all the members of His Body that are gathered together

13

in Him shall follow in His train. There the glorious King shall reign in them, and they in Him. And they shall receive the kingdom of eternal bliss as their inheritance that was prepared for them even before the world was created.

We cannot know what that kingdom will be like, and so how can we write about it? But this I know for sure, and I make so bold as to say—that you will lack nothing that you desire, and you will not have anything that you would rather be without. There shall be no weeping nor wailing, no sorrow nor dread, no discord nor envy, no tribulation nor temptation. There will be no such thing as corruption, suspicion, or ambition; no such thing as the sickness of old age, death, or poverty; no trace of need or weariness or faintness. And where none of these things is to be found, what else may there be but perfect joy and mirth and peace; perfect security, and unmarred love and charity; perfect riches, beauty, and rest; health and strength and the perfect sight of God? And in that everlasting and perpetual life what more could you want?

God our creator will be clearly seen, known, and loved. He will be seen in Himself as He reigns in perfect bliss. He will be seen in His creatures as He governs and rules all things without the least trouble or toil, as He keeps all things unwearyingly, and as He gives Himself to all things in the measure that they can receive Him, without any lessening of His Godhead. The face of God that the angels desire to gaze upon shall be seen in all its sweetness, lovableness, and desirability. But who may speak of the clearness and brightness of that vision?

There shall we see the Father in the Son, the Son in the

Father, and the Holy Ghost in them both. There God our creator will be seen, not as in a mirror or in darkness, but face to face, as the Gospel says. There God will be seen as He is, when the promise that He made in the Gospel is fulfilled: "Who loves me shall be loved by my Father, and I shall love him and show him my own self." And it is from this clear sight of Him that that blissful knowledge comes of which Christ speaks in the Gospel: "This is eternal life, that they may know Thee, the one true God, and Jesus Christ whom Thou didst send."

From this knowledge there springs so great a fervor of blissful desire, so much fullness of love, so much sweetness of charity, that the completeness of bliss may not take away the joyful desire, nor may the desire stand in the way of completeness. And how can we say all this in a few words? Surely, sister, it is in this way: "Eye hath not seen, nor ear heard, what God has made ready for those who love Him."[1]

Heaven on Earth

Bliss—great joy and happiness—this Christ has promised to us for eternity. Yet we often wonder, is there joy for us here on earth? His saints tell us yes.

The knowledge that heaven awaits us is in itself a great cause for joy. The Venerable Thecla Merlo used to remind her sisters:

There are difficulties, sufferings, and worries…. But one beautiful day it will be all over, and we will find ourselves all united in heaven with the Blessed Trinity, with Mary most holy, with our dear ones and with the Sisters who have gone before us. This is our joy and our comfort. Courage!

St. Aelred attributes the joy of heaven not only to having our every desire satisfied but also to seeing God face-to-face. The lives of the saints attest to the fact that the union with God that we are able to achieve on this earth is a sure guarantee of deep and abiding joy here.

> The heart is rich when it is content, and it is always content when its desires are fixed on God. Nothing can bring greater happiness than doing God's will for the love of God.
>
> *Blessed Br. Miguel Febres Cordero, F.S.C.*

Mary, Model of Joy

What better model for heavenly joy can we find than our Blessed Mother? Her great *fiat* is the ultimate expression of surrender to God's will. Thus she welcomed into her own person Jesus, the very Person of God and source of all joy.

Mary, Queen of All Saints, leads us in joy as she does in sorrow.

Rejoice heartily, O daughter Zion, shout for joy, O daughter Jerusalem! See, your king shall come to you; a just savior is he.

ZECHARIAH 9:9

The Seven Joys of the Blessed Virgin Mary

A devotion begun in the Middle Ages celebrates seven joyful events in the life of Our Lady.

The Annunciation

The young Jewish girl received with joy the news that the Savior of the world was coming, the King whose kingdom would have no end. Her response was her *fiat*, her definitive "yes."

> Sing and rejoice, O daughter Zion! See, I am coming to dwell among you, says the Lord.
>
> ZECHARIAH 2:14

To be chosen from all women, to know that she would forever be called blessed, to provide the womb for the man-God, what privilege was given to the humble virgin!

> Let us rejoice and be glad and give him glory. For the wedding day of the Lamb has come, his bride has made herself ready.
>
> REVELATION 19:7

The Visitation

Mary, hearing of the pregnancy of her cousin Elizabeth, hastened to visit her and to offer her aid. Elizabeth, filled with the Holy Spirit, cried out a greeting and a blessing to Mary.

> Most blessed are you among women…. The moment the sound of your greeting reached my ears, the infant in my womb leaped for joy. Blessed are you who believed that what was spoken to you … by the Lord would be fulfilled.
>
> LUKE 1:42-45

And Mary answered Elizabeth, "My spirit finds joy in God my savior" (Lk 1:47), then went on to praise God for all the good He brings to His people. Full of love and of life, the cousins visited happily in anticipation.

The Nativity

When her time had come, Mary brought forth her firstborn Son. No royal crib for a bed, tenderly she wrapped Him in swaddling clothes and laid him in a manger. The warm breath of the ox and the ass, the sweet smell of the hay, and the gentle baby sounds of this God-made-Man filled the stable. What silent joys must have invaded the hearts of Mary and Joseph as they gazed at the tiny Babe. A multitude of the heavenly host heralded His coming; humble shepherds came to honor Him.

The Adoration of the Magi

Wise men from the East "were overjoyed at seeing the star" (Mt 2:10). Falling down before the infant King, they presented gifts of gold and frankincense and myrrh. How Mary's heart must have swelled to see her infant son bringing joy to poor and rich alike.

The Finding of Jesus in the Temple

The Babe grew in the humble, loving home at Nazareth. Under the watchful eyes of Joseph and Mary, His uncertain, toddling steps became sure-footed strides; His chubby legs grew straight and strong. At last, when Jesus was twelve, He went with His parents to Jerusalem according to the custom of the feast. Mary and Joseph set out on the return trip, thinking Jesus was in the company. After a day's journey they sought

Him, and when they did not find Him, they returned to Jerusalem.

This is an incident counted as both a sorrow and a joy for Mary. How often the two come together. Mary and Joseph sought Jesus for three days. Imagine the joy of the mother on finding Him! Yet how piercing His words: "Why were you looking for Me? Did you not know that I must be in My Father's house?" (Lk 2:49-50).

The Appearance of the Risen Lord

The path to joy leads through the cross. There Mary stoically kept vigil. She held her dead son in her arms, then placed Him in the tomb. A great flood of sorrow washed over the virgin. And yet, how much greater was her joy when she met Him again, resurrected from the dead! God freed Him and raised Him up; death could not keep its hold on Him.

Therefore my heart is glad, my soul rejoices;
my body also dwells secure,
for you will not abandon me to Sheol, nor let your faithful
servant see the pit.
You will show me the path to life,
abounding joy in your presence,
the delights at your right hand forever.

PSALM 16:9-11

The Assumption and Coronation of Mary, Queen of Heaven

At last the King called His beloved to ascend higher.

A great sign appeared in the sky, a woman clothed with the sun, with the moon under her feet, and on her head a crown of twelve stars.

REVELATION 12:1

The Queen of All Saints leads us with joy, through the cross, to joy everlasting.

TWO

No Sad Saints!

From somber, serious, sullen saints, save us, O Lord.
St. Teresa of Avila

St. Teresa of Avila, foundress of the reformed ("Discalced") Carmelites, was known for her ironic sense of humor and a deft ability to turn a phrase. In spite of times of darkness, depression, and spiritual aridity, Teresa maintained a smiling countenance and her wonderful sense of humor.

This great reformer and mystic had much of the comedian in her personality from the time of her childhood. The young Spanish girl told her father that she thought the martyrs were "smart" because "they got to heaven right away." She and her young brother attempted to run away and become martyrs, but the plan failed when their uncle discovered them and immediately returned them home.

There was no short path to heaven for Teresa. In the last twenty-five years of her life she wrote a number of books, poems, and letters. Her sense of humor bubbles up through her writings, which are still studied with interest today. She was declared a Doctor of the Church in 1970.

A depressed sister once accused herself with some pride of being a great sinner. Teresa rejoined, "Sister, remember, none of us is perfect. Just make sure those sins of yours don't turn into bad habits." Another time a difficult abbess was getting on Teresa's nerves. Teresa prayed, "Lord, if I had my way that woman wouldn't be superior here." She wrote that the Lord answered her, "Teresa, if I had My way, she wouldn't be, either."

Then we have the favorite anecdote of Teresa's conversation with God after a nearly disastrous trip. Teresa complained, "Lord, I prayed to You for a safe and pleasant trip, and what do I get? I get nothing but problems."

God replied, "But Teresa, that's how I treat all My friends."

Teresa immediately rejoined, "Yes, I know, and that's why You've got so few of them!"

Holy Camaraderie

In the lives and legends of even the earliest of the saints we read instances of holy joy and humor. St. Benedict and St. Scholastica were twins, children of Christian patricians. Scholastica (which means "scholar" or "disciple") was probably given this name because she was her brother's scholar in his "School of the Lord's Service," as he termed the monastic life.

Little is known of their early lives, but many legends have grown up around the pair. St. Scholastica apparently had a joyous nature and lived simply in an intense mystical union with God. There is a tradition that she founded a community of nuns at Plombariola, about five miles from Benedict's monastery, although no historical documents or ruins remain to confirm its location.

According to the writings of St. Gregory, it was customary for St. Benedict and St. Scholastica to meet once a year at a house about halfway between the monastery and the convent. There they would spend a day together in prayer and spiritual conversation. This was an occasion of mutual encouragement and support.

On the last of these occasions, the saintly pair had spent the day as usual and together with their companions had just finished their evening meal. The time for parting was at hand, and Scholastica, perhaps sensing her impending death, asked her brother to continue the discussion and postpone his return to the monastery until the next morning. Disciplined monk that he was, Benedict refused.

Scholastica was determined not to let her brother go easily. Bowing her head, she prayed that God would answer her petition. As soon as she raised her head, a torrential storm began, making it impossible for Benedict and his monks to leave.

In astonishment, Benedict looked at his sister and asked, "What have you done?"

Laughingly Scholastica replied, "I asked a favor of you, and you refused. I asked my Lord, and He has granted my petition. Go now, brother! Go if you can!"

Benedict had no alternative but to yield to his sister's wishes. They resumed their discourse, spending the entire night in delightful conversation on spiritual things.

Three days later Benedict understood more clearly the significance of this miracle. God favored him with a vision in which he saw the soul of his sister winging its way to heaven in the form of a dove. He announced the death to his community, thanking God for the eternal happiness of his sister. Benedict arranged for Scholastica's burial in the tomb he had prepared for himself, and where he himself was laid only a few weeks later. In death, as in life, brother and sister remained closely united.

Joy of Human Friendship

St. Augustine, the great saint and Doctor of the Church, was drawn to the beauty of the present and grounded to it through his love of "Him who is everywhere present." He recognized the joy that human friendships can provide, and with his friends he struggled to reconcile love for the pleasures of this world with love of God.

> What attached me most to my friends was the pleasure of talking and laughing with them, to read with them the same books, to joke and talk nonsense, sometimes to argue but without anger, and thus to emphasize the pleasure of generally agreeing; to miss an absent friend, to welcome his return. We loved each other with all our hearts; these friendships were expressed by our eyes, our gesture, our voices.[1]

Rejoice Always!

St. Francis of Assisi, born in 1182, was a unique person with a positive genius and passion for loving God. His love of God was a source of ecstatic joy, which became a characteristic mark of the saint and his followers and has appealed to millions throughout the centuries.

Francis could not tolerate about him those who were sad or melancholy; for him, sadness and moroseness were signs of hypocrisy and sin.

It is not fitting that a servant of God should offer to men the spectacle of sadness and trouble, but rather one of constant cheerfulness.[2]

Francis did not confuse sadness with suffering. Suffering could even be a source of joy if it helped one to conform to Christ.

* * *

We find a great example of joy in suffering in the Polish priest St. Maximilian Kolbe. In a childhood encounter with Our Lady, he had accepted the crown of martyrdom. He suffered brutal persecution at the hands of the Nazis. Yet he wrote, "If you only knew how happy I am! My heart is full of that peace and joy which can be experienced even here on earth. Yes, in spite of the anxieties and worries of each day, at the bottom of my heart is always a peace and joy I can't describe." Kolbe willingly gave his life in exchange for the life of a fellow prisoner at Auschwitz.

The saintly student activist Blessed Pier Giorgio Frassati explained his cheerfulness during his fatal illness:

You ask me whether I am cheerful. How could I not be, so long as my trust in God gives me strength? We should always be cheerful. Sadness should be banished from all Christian souls. For suffering is a far different thing from sadness, which is the worst disease of all. It is almost always caused by lack of faith. But the purpose for which we have been created shows us the path along which we should tread, perhaps strewn with many thorns, but not a sad path. Even in the midst of intense suffering it is one of joy.[3]

* * *

The beloved foundress of the Cenacle Sisters, St. Therese Couderc, put a great emphasis on mortification and abnegation. Yet she found no place in the Christian life for sadness. She would say to the young religious, "We should never allow even one thought of sadness to enter the soul. Have we not within us Him who is the joy of heaven! Believe me when I say that an obedient religious is a happy religious."

* * *

Our own native American Blessed Kateri Tekakwitha, the Mohawk maiden, is described by her biographer, Fr. Cholenc, as "always gay, always content." He wrote that the other Indians liked to be near her in chapel "so that they could pray better." He found her cheerful attitude surprising because gaiety was not a characteristic normally found among the Mohawks, who generally maintained a solemn demeanor. Kateri kept her happy nature even through her final months of great suffering from illness. She died at the age of twenty-three in 1680.

The Joy of Repentance

One saint who suffered greatly but eventually found joy was the French actress Eve Lavallière. As a child Eve escaped into fantasy from the alcohol-induced violence and abuse of her home life. Finally her mother separated from her father, and things seemed to get better. One day, however, her father wheedled an invitation to come for dinner.

The peaceful meal soon turned violent. Eve was standing on the balcony when she heard a shot. She returned inside to find her mother with a face full of blood. Her father turned his pistol toward her, but something stopped him. He turned the gun on himself, killing himself instantly. Eve's mother died three weeks later.

The eighteen-year-old orphan went on to a glorious career on the stage as one of France's top comediennes. She became the mistress of a marquis and then of a theatrical promoter, by whom she bore an illegitimate daughter. She had several other notorious affairs. Men showered her with money, furs, and jewels, but neither these nor her fame brought her happiness. Her daughter became a lesbian and flaunted her lifestyle in front of her mother.

At last, soul weary, exhausted, and depressed to the point of suicide, Eve rented a château in the country for a summer's rest. Here she met a village priest who became the instrument of her conversion and her return to the faith. Although he advised her that she could be a good actress and a good Christian, she determined to give up acting and become a penitent. She spent some time near Lourdes and later in North Africa, where she worked with a lay missionary nursing team.

She practiced stern austerities and took a vow of poverty. At last, her fragile health ruined, she retired to a small French villa she named Bethany.

Eve told a friend that, in spite of her hardships, physical suffering, and periods of darkness and depression, her new life brought her a happiness she had never known at any time before. She joined the Third Order Secular of St. Francis and began a daily routine in which she seriously lived out her commitment.

In 1928 Eve developed a bad case of peritonitis, running high fevers, unable to sleep, and in constant pain. Her wayward daughter came to assist in her care, and secretly gave Eve cocaine to help her relax and sleep well. After a few days, Eve developed an addiction to it. When the doctor discovered what had happened, he sent Eve's daughter away, but was forced to keep Eve on a maintenance dose of the drug until her death a year and a half later. Although hers was a long and difficult illness, she accepted it with joy, offering her suffering in reparation. She told a friend, "When people mention me to you, make it quite clear to them, all those who know me, that you have seen the happiest, indeed the most perfectly happy of women."

* * *

Another modern penitent who found true joy was the alcoholic Irish workingman Matt Talbot. He came home drunk for the first time at the age of twelve, the day he got his first job in a wine-bottling establishment. After that he was drunk daily. He spent all his time outside of work in rowdy bars, often finagling money to buy the liquor his body craved.

At last, at the age of twenty-eight, Matt determined to take the pledge of abstinence. An expert mason's assistant, he spent his remaining forty-one years in manual labor, secretly doing penance. Of his fasting he said, "We do well to punish the body and not be studying the gut." It was only at his death that people discovered the heavy penitential chains he wore around his waist, arm, and knee.

As his spirituality advanced, Matt became quieter and avoided doing anything to mark himself. He was always good-humored and would join in conversations about sports and other earthly things in order to be sociable. He earned the respect of his fellow workers, who considered him a "regular guy."

After paying his rent and buying the little food he needed, Matt would distribute the rest of his wages to charity. He collapsed and died on his way to Mass at the age of sixty-nine.

The Perpetual Jubilee

St. Theophane Venard was a youthful priest of the Paris Foreign Mission Society who was beheaded in Hanoi in 1861. He was a favorite of St. Thérèse of Lisieux, who wrote a hymn in his honor and requested one of his relics as she neared death. She said, "He is a little saint. There is nothing out of the ordinary in his life. He loved the immaculate Virgin very much, his family, too. And so do I. I cannot understand those saints who did not."

Possibly the best known of the Vietnam martyrs, Theophane's fascinating letters, especially those written from the bamboo cage where he was jailed for the last two months of his life, have inspired generations of French missionaries. He wrote to his family:

> Can you fancy me sitting quietly in the center of my wooden cage, borne by eight soldiers in the midst of an immense crowd?... I hear some of them say, "What a pretty boy that European is! He is gay and bright as if he were going to a feast."

St. Theophane was well aware that he was, indeed, going to the Great Feast that lay on the other side of the cross of his martyrdom. He advised, "Be merry, really merry. The life of a true Christian should be a perpetual jubilee, a prelude to the festivals of eternity."

> Love is itself the fulfillment of all our works. There is the goal; that is why we run: we run toward it, and once we reach it, in it we shall find rest.
>
> *St. Augustine*

Finding Our Joy

How do we find this joy? We can contemplate the blessing of faith, the beginning of eternal life. We can recognize our utter dependence with respect to the Creator; this is a source of wisdom, freedom, joy, and confidence. We can strive to acquire human virtue, which disposes us for communion with divine love and thus makes possible our joy.

The path to joy passes by way of the cross. Renunciation and spiritual battle are found along the road. Gradually, through the cross, we live in the peace and joy of the Beatitudes. And we can meet, listen to, make friends with, and imitate the saints who found joy. There are no sad saints.

THREE

Finding Perfect Joy

We should wish for nothing else and have no other desire; we should find no pleasure or delight in anything except in our Creator, Redeemer, and Savior; he alone is true God, who is perfect good.... Through him and in him is all pardon, all grace, and all glory for the penitent, the just, and the blessed who rejoice in heaven.

St. Francis of Assisi

Throughout history, no other name has been more synonymous with joy than that of the gentle "Poverello," St. Francis Bernadone. Born in Assisi, Italy, the son of a wealthy silk merchant, Francis spent his early years as a pleasure-seeking popular leader of the youth of his town. After three years as a soldier, he experienced visions and went on pilgrimage to Rome. When he returned home, he was denounced as a lunatic and publicly disinherited by his father. He then went to the church of San Damiano, which he repaired with the help of friends. In the small chapel known as the Portiuncula, he dedicated himself to the care of the poor.

The Franciscan Order was founded in 1209 and received approval the following year from Pope Innocent III. St. Clare had joined St. Francis in 1212, founding the cloistered Poor

Clares as part of the Franciscan family. There were five thousand Franciscans at the order's general chapter meeting in 1219. Francis sent friars throughout Europe and to the Middle East, and the new fraternity, known as the Friars Minor, spread like wildfire.

In 1224, while praying on Mount Alvernia, Francis received the sacred stigmata, visible symbols of the wounds of Christ in his own flesh. He died two years later and was canonized in 1228.

Joyous worship, reverence for nature, and concern for the sick and poor characterized the life of this humble saint. Even today his followers in the Franciscan Order keep this charism of joy wherever they serve throughout the world.

The Little Flowers

Many stories are told of the "Seraphic father," as Francis was called. His early biographers report his advice about spiritual joy. One account tells how the joys of the saint sometimes turned to tears: [1]

> Drunken with the love and compassion of Christ,... the most sweet melody of spirit boiling up within him frequently broke out in French speech, and the veins of murmuring, which he heard secretly with his ears, broke forth into French-like rejoicing. And sometimes he picked up a branch from the earth, and laying it on his left arm he drew in his right hand another stick like a bow over it, as if on a violin or other instrument, and making fitting gestures, sang with it in French unto the Lord Jesus Christ. But all this playing ended

in tears, and this joy dissolved in compassion for the Passion of Christ. In these times he would draw sighs continually; and with deep drawn groans, forgetful of those things which he held in his hands, he was raised to heaven.

"The Blessed father," as the author calls Francis, aspired to continual "spiritual gladness." To this he exhorted his brothers also:

If the servant of God would study to preserve within and without the spiritual joy which comes of cleanness of heart and is acquired by devoutness of prayer, the demons would not be able to harm him, for they would say, "Since this servant of God has joy in tribulation as in prosperity, we can find no way of entering into him nor of hurting him." But the demons exult when they can quench or hinder in any way the devotion and joy which arises from prayer and other virtuous works....

Since, therefore, my brethren, this spiritual joy comes of cleanness of heart and the purity of continual prayer, ye should be first and foremost desirous to acquire and conserve these two things, that ye may have, within and without, that joy which with the greatest longing I desire and wish to know and feel in you and myself to the edification of our neighbors and the reproach of the enemy. For it pertaineth to him and to his members to grow sad, but to you ever to rejoice and be glad in the Lord.

Even sorrow for sin should not dim one's countenance, Francis said. He exhorted one long-faced penitent:

Why dost thou make an outward show of sorrow and sadness for thy offences? Keep thou this sadness between thee and thy God, and pray to Him that by His mercy He may spare thee, and restore to thy soul the gladness of His salvation, which is taken away from thee on account of sin, but before me and others, study always to have joy, for it befits not the servant of God to show before his brother or another sadness or a troubled face.

This is not to say that Francis encouraged laughter and idle words. Such were often signs not of spiritual gladness but rather "vanity and folly." And while he did not approve a melancholy face, he did admire and encourage "gravity and modesty of manners," which he said were a protection against the wiles of the devil. Of what, then, does the "joy of the servant of God" consist?

Blessed is that religious who has no joy nor gladness except in the most holy words and works of the Lord and with these provokes man to the love of the Lord in joy and gladness. And woe to that religious who rejoices in idle and vain words, and with these provokes men to laughter.

What Is Perfect Joy?

There is a well-loved tale from *The Little Flowers* in which St. Francis tries to teach Friar Leo a lesson about the joy of the cross. Francis and Friar Leo are traveling to visit their brothers at St. Mary of the Angels. Both of them are suffering sorely from the bitter cold.

First Francis tells Leo what is not perfect joy: the friars' good examples of holiness and edification; the ability to work miracles of healing and casting out devils; spiritual gifts such as speaking in tongues and the gifts of knowledge and eloquent preaching. After two miles of this type of talk, Friar Leo asks in great wonder, "Father, prithee in God's name tell me where is perfect joy to be found?" So St. Francis answers:

If, when we shall arrive at St. Mary of the Angels, all drenched with rain and trembling with cold, all covered with mud and exhausted from hunger; if, when we knock at the convent gate, the porter should come angrily and ask us who we are; if, after we have told him, "We are two of the brethren," he should answer angrily, "What you say is not the truth; you are but two impostors going about to deceive the world, and take away the alms of the poor; begone, I say"; if then he should refuse to open to us, and leave us outside, exposed to the snow and rain, suffering from cold and hunger till night fall then, if we accept such injustice, such cruelty and such contempt with patience, without being ruffled and without murmuring, believing with humility and charity that the porter really knows us, and that it is God who makes him to speak thus against us, write down, O Brother Leo, that this is perfect joy.

And if we should knock again, and the porter should come out in anger to drive us away with oaths and blows, as if we were vile impostors, saying, "Begone, miserable robbers! to the hospital, for here you shall neither eat nor sleep"; and if we accept all this with patience, with joy, and with charity, O Brother Leo, write that this indeed is perfect joy.

And if, urged by cold and hunger, we should knock again, calling to the porter and entreating him with many tears to open to us and give us shelter, for the love of God, and if he should come out more angry than before, exclaiming, "These are but importunate rascals, I will deal with them as they deserve"; and taking a knotted stick, he should seize us by the hood, throwing us on the ground, rolling us in the snow, and beat and wound us with the knots in the stick; if we bear all these injuries with patience and joy, thinking of the sufferings of our Blessed Lord, which we would share out of love for him, write, O Brother Leo, that here, finally, is perfect joy.

And now, brother, listen to the conclusion. Above all the graces and all the gifts of the Holy Spirit that Christ grants to his friends, is the grace of overcoming oneself, and accepting willingly, out of love for Christ, all suffering, injury, discomfort and contempt. For in all other gifts of God we cannot glory, seeing that they proceed not from ourselves but from God, according to the words of the apostle: "What do you have that you have not received from God? And if you have received it, why do you glory as if you had not received it?" [1 Cor 4:7]. But in the cross of tribulation and affliction we may glory, because, as the apostle says again, "I will not glory save in the cross of our Lord Jesus Christ [Gal 6:14]."

Joy to the World!

While St. Francis gloried in the cross, he also understood and gloried in nature. He had discovered that all creation belongs to God, and this made him brother to all God's other creatures. The world was one big joyful family for Francis.

Today we have reminders of Francis' joy in some of the beautiful Christmas customs that have been passed on to us. The custom of being especially kind to animals and allowing them to share in the joy of Christmas comes to us from Francis. He admonished farmers to give their stock extra corn and hay at Christmas "for reverence of the Son of God, whom on such a night the blessed Virgin Mary did lay down in the stall between the ox and the ass."

Francis believed that all creation should rejoice at Christmas especially, and the dumb creatures had no other means of doing so except by enjoying more comfort and better food. "If I could see the Emperor," he said, "I would implore him to issue a general decree that all people who are able to do so shall throw grain and corn upon the streets, so that on this great feast day the birds might have enough to eat, especially our sisters the larks."

St. Francis was the first to introduce the joyous carol spirit that spread all over Europe and later to the New World. He had a particular devotion and affection for the mysteries of the holy childhood of Jesus. Thomas of Celano, St. Francis' biographer, wrote, "The Child Jesus was forgotten by the hearts of many, but with the grace of God He was resurrected again and recalled to loving memory in those hearts through His servant, the Blessed Francis."

St. Francis wrote a beautiful Christmas hymn in Latin, and his companions and spiritual sons contributed a number of lovely Italian Christmas carols. One of these thirteenth-century Italian carols points out the joy of its early Franciscan author:

> In Bethlehem is born the Holy Child,
> On hay and straw in the winter wild,
> O, my heart is full of mirth
> At Jesus' birth.

The image of the Child in the manger and various other graphic representations of the nativity have been used in church services from the first centuries. The crèche tradition is credited to St. Francis, who made the Christmas crib popular through his famous celebration at Greccio, Italy, on Christmas Eve 1223. His Bethlehem scene included live animals. Francis declared that he wanted to see with his own eyes "how poor and miserable He wished to be for our sake."

At midnight the brothers and the folk of the countryside came together, and Mass was said with the manger as an altar, so that the Divine Child under the forms of bread and wine should Himself come to the place. Francis arrived and rejoiced. Greccio had become a new Bethlehem. The saint, dressed in deacons' vestments (Francis was never a priest), sang the Gospel and preached a delightful sermon.

The Song of Brother Sun

Francis' health declined during the final three years of his life. He was subject to many infirmities and afflicted with constant pain. He ordered the brothers to sing the praises of the Lord frequently, both day and night. Brother Elias, seeing how Francis rejoiced in the midst of such sickness, rebuked him, telling him that the people of the town might question why he was so joyful and lighthearted. They might feel he should be thinking of his death.

Francis told Brother Elias that he daily considered the day of his death. Then he pleaded, "Allow me, Brother, to rejoice in the Lord, both in His praises and in my infirmities, since by the grace of the Holy Spirit helping me, I am so united and joined to my Lord that by His mercy may I well rejoice in the Most High."

Francis asked his doctor for the truth about his illness. The doctor admitted that Francis was incurable, whereupon Francis said with great joy of mind and body, "Welcome, my Sister Death."

Then the holy Francis called to him Br. Angelo and Br. Leo and asked them to sing to him the "Song of Brother Sun," which Francis himself had written. Before the last verse of the canticle he added some verses for Sister Death. This joyful canticle of this most joyful of saints has survived to our day. With Francis, we can praise the Lord in *all* creation.

Most High, Omnipotent, Good Lord.
Thine be the praise, the glory,
   the honor, and all benediction.

To Thee alone, Most High, they are due,
And no man is worthy to mention Thee.

Be Thou praised, my Lord, with all Thy creatures,
Above all Brother Sun,
Who gives the day and lightens us therewith.

And he is beautiful and radiant with great splendor,
Of Thee, Most High, he bears similitude.

Be Thou praised, my Lord,
   of Sister Moon and the stars,
In the heaven hast Thou formed them,
Clear and precious and comely.

Be Thou praised, my Lord, of Brother Wind,
And of the air, and the cloud and of fair and of all weather,
By the which Thou givest to Thy creatures sustenance.

Be Thou praised, my Lord, of Sister Water,
Which is much useful and humble and precious and pure.

Be Thou praised, my Lord, of Brother Fire,
By which Thou hast lightened the night,
And he is beautiful and joyful and robust and strong.

Be Thou praised, my Lord, of our Sister Mother Earth,
Which sustains and governs us
And produces divers fruits with colored flowers and herbs.

Be Thou praised, my Lord,
   of those who pardon for Thy love
And endure sickness and tribulations.

Blessed are they who will endure it in peace,
For by Thee, Most High, they shall be crowned.

Be Thou praised, my Lord, of our Sister Bodily Death,
From whom no man living may escape.
Woe to those who die in mortal sin.

Blessed are they who are found in Thy most holy will,
For the second death shall not work them ill.

Praise ye and bless my Lord, and give Him thanks,
And serve Him with great humility.

FOUR

Fools for Christ

God chose the foolish of the world to shame the wise, and God chose the weak of the world to shame the strong.

1 CORINTHIANS 1:27

We are fools on Christ's account, but you are wise in Christ.

1 CORINTHIANS 4:10a

What is a holy fool—a fool for Christ? Simply someone who does not operate out of conventional wisdom, which often dictates conformity, but rather follows the radical directives of the gospel.

The Apostle Paul advised his fellow Christians to cultivate the foolishness of spiritual life. The Desert Fathers enthusiastically followed his advice in the third and fourth centuries. Paul and the ascetics later inspired generations of spiritual radicals in the Church.

Dry Wit From the Desert

The earliest Christian monks inhabited the desert land of Syria, Egypt, and Palestine from the end of the second century

45

onwards. Known as the "Desert Fathers," the lives of these ascetic hermits and cenobites are the foundation upon which the great Western monastic tradition was built. These hermits often went to extremes in their strenuous pursuit of spiritual rigor. We can fairly call them "athletes for Christ" for their seeming competition in feats of endurance.

About the end of the third century, St. Anthony of Egypt oversaw a group of five thousand monks. These men, who were searching for salvation and unity with God, were often sought for spiritual guidance. Emperor Constantine was among those who appealed to St. Anthony for his counsel.

Many of the stories from the Desert Fathers have been preserved. These early ascetics had some wonderful insights into the human condition, and sometimes their anecdotes display a wit as dry as their surroundings.

When Anthony went to the mountain fort near what is now Deir el Memum, he took up a solitary residence. Local supporters threw food over the walls, keeping him alive, but for twenty years he did not see a human face. Slowly, other ascetics built a community in huts and nearby caves, and they begged Anthony to come out of seclusion to direct their prayers and observances. He did, and later he moved to a monastery in the desert. Here he was a friend of St. Paul of Thebes, called "the Hermit," who was reputedly fed by ravens who brought him half a loaf of bread a day. When Anthony came to visit, the ravens brought a full loaf.

Even in Anthony's day, those who chose to be "different" were often reviled or attacked. His wise and humorous counsel about this spans the centuries: "The time is coming when people will be insane, and when they see someone who is not insane, they will attack that person saying, 'You are insane because you are not like us.'"

One day a group came with Abba Joseph to see the saint. In order to test them, he read a text from Scripture and, beginning with the youngest, asked them to explain the text he had read. Each of the group gave an opinion, but to each one Abba Anthony replied, "You have not understood it." Finally he asked Abba Joseph to explain the Scripture, and Abba Joseph replied, "I do not know." Then, finishing his lesson in humility, Abba Anthony said, "Indeed, Abba Joseph has found the way, for he has said, 'I do not know.'"

Oddly Joyful

These desert saints sometimes seemed an odd group. Their number included the two Simeon Stylites, who lived most of their lives at the top of a pillar; mystics such as Arsenius, a recluse who refused to allow people to see his face; John the Short, who in obedience to his superior watered a walking stick, which sprouted; and John of Egypt, who had himself walled up in a hermitage with a single window through which he preached to the public on Sundays. Abba Agatho conceived a unique tool to teach himself silence; for three years he carried a stone in his mouth until he learned the lesson.

Moses the Black, born into slavery, was driven out of his Egyptian master's estate because of his violence and evil. He became the leader of a vicious outlaw band and hid from the authorities in the desert of Skete. There he was converted to God and became a monk, eventually coming to enjoy many supernatural and mystical gifts.

Moses built a hermitage in the desert, where he hoped to

lose himself in contemplation. Disciples began to come to him for his wise counsel. Once a brother came to see him and begged him for a word. The old monk advised him, "Go and sit in your cell, and your cell will teach you everything."

Another time one of the brothers committed a sin, so the elders assembled and to judge him sent for Abba Moses. Moses, however, did not want to go. The priest then sent him a message saying "Come, everybody is waiting for you."

So Moses got up to go, but he took with him a worn-out basket filled with sand. As the brothers came out to meet him, they saw the sand flowing out of the holes in the basket and asked, "What is this?"

Abba Moses replied, "My sins are running out behind me, yet I do not see them. And today I have come to judge the sins of someone else." Filled with shame by the example of the wise old monk, the brothers pardoned their sinful colleague.

A dog is better than I am because a dog also has love, but unlike I myself, the dog does not pass judgment.

Abba Xanthias

If wishing to correct another you are moved to anger, you gratify your own passion. Do not lose yourself in order to save another.

Abbot Macarius

Desert Wisdom

The Abbot Macarius used to say to the brethren in Skete, "When Mass is ended in the church, flee, my brothers." One of the brethren said to him, "Father, whither in this solitude can we further flee?" And he laid his finger upon his mouth saying, "This is what I would have you flee." Then the saintly abbot retired alone to his cell and shut the door.

Abba Doulas was the disciple of Abba Bessarion. He explained to one of the brothers how his mentor had taught him a lesson about faith:

> When we were walking along the sea one day, I was thirsty so I said to Abba Bessarion, "Abba, I am very thirsty."
>
> Then he prayed and said to me, "Then drink from the sea."
>
> And the water was sweet when I drank it. So I poured it into a flask so that I would not be thirsty later. Seeing this, he asked me, "Why are you doing that!"
>
> And I answered, "So that I won't be thirsty later on."
>
> Then Abba Bessarion replied, "God is here and God is everywhere."

In 407, when barbarian raiders destroyed the Egyptian monastic settlement at Skete, one survivor was Abbot Poemen. About one fourth of the sayings and stories in the *Apophthegmata Patrum* (*Sayings of the Fathers*), one of the most influential works of early Christian monasticism, are attributed to him.

Abba Poemen once told a fellow monk: "Remember the words of the old men, and you will find help in them and you will be saved."

The Joy of Desert Mothers

Some women hermits also found the solitude of the desert their opportunity to draw close to God. One such woman was Syncletica, the daughter of wealthy Macedonians, born in Alexandria, Egypt. Refusing all offers of marriage, she gave away her wealth on the deaths of her parents. With her blind sister, she retired to a life of austere seclusion in an empty tomb. She suffered from temptations and severe spiritual dryness. In her later years she patiently endured many other trials, including cancer.

Sought out for her wise spiritual advice, gently she explained the joy of seeking enlightenment.

In the beginning there is a struggle and a lot of work for those who come near to God. But after that, there is indescribable joy. It is just like building a fire; at first it's smoky and your eyes water, but later you get the desired result. Thus, we ought to light the divine fire in ourselves with tears and effort.

To many, these ascetics—men and women alike—represent at best a quaint oddity from our past. The Church acknowledges their presence, like that of an eccentric relative, though she does not encourage our imitating them. The modern monk and spiritual writer Thomas Merton is one who appreciated the spirituality of these early desert dwellers. His book *Wisdom of the Desert* can help the modern reader understand it too. We can all enjoy the lessons taught with wit and wisdom by these holy people.

The Holy Fool

In the Orthodox tradition the holy fool was an individual who chose to behave publicly in a bizarre and foolish manner, while in reality living a saintly and ascetic life. In the tenth century St. Andrew the Fool adopted the life of a seemingly insane beggar, roaming the streets nearly naked and sleeping under the open sky in the company of wild dogs.

Also of this tradition is St. Symeon the Fool, one of the most colorful of the early Christian saints. He spent years living on lentils in an isolated cave, struggling against temptation, as did many of his fellow ascetics. Then he decided to play the fool in order to mock the world and conceal his identity as a saint.

Symeon seems a bizarre choice for the title *Saint*, since it is through very peculiar antics that he converted heretics and reformed sinners. He walked about naked, ate enormous quantities of beans, and once tied a dead dog to his belt, dragging it along as he entered the city of Emesa in Syria. His behavior was not only eccentric but scandalous. He threw nuts at the clergy and blew out the candles in church. He feasted on fast days and danced in inappropriate places.

Only after Symeon's death did his secret sanctity come to light. He had performed many acts of kindness, as well as some strange and wonderful miracles.

* * *

About the eleventh century a number of these holy fools appeared in Russia and the Slavic regions. In later centuries these saints played a significant historical role. St. Nicholas Salos stood up to Ivan the Terrible, and St. Ivan Big-Cap confronted Czar Boris Godunov, incidents immortalized in a popular opera. Eventually the holy fool type became well-known to all Russians, forming a philosophical basis for Dostoyevsky's novel *The Idiot.*

* * *

Belgium has its own saintly eccentric. St. Christina the Astonishing (or Mirabilis) was born in Liège about the year 1150 and was orphaned at the age of three. When she was twenty-one she had a sort of seizure and seemed to have died. At her funeral Mass she suddenly soared to the roof of the church. The priest ordered her to come down. She did, then told him that she had been to hell, purgatory, and heaven and was allowed to return to earth to pray for the suffering souls in purgatory.

Many people considered Christina insane; others venerated her. She could not tolerate the odor of sinful human beings and resorted to extraordinary means to escape human contact, such as climbing trees and soaring to the rafters in churches. Living in poverty, she camped out even in the winter, often on icy rivers. She ran naked through thorns, provoking neighborhood dogs to chase her.

Christina's spiritual experiences were truly extraordinary. She possessed prophetic gifts and often underwent out-of-body experiences. In moments of quiet prayer, she became as shapeless as "hot wax," then curled up like a hedgehog before resuming her human form. She lived her final years at St. Catherine Convent at St.-Trond, where she died in 1224.

The Love of a Fool

Blessed Xenia of St. Petersburg, who died in 1805, has become the favorite holy fool among the Orthodox faithful. Xenia was a young woman, probably from the lesser nobility, when her husband died suddenly at a drinking party. She realized the vanity of earthly treasures and went on to discover that real joy is found only in Christ. She distributed all her possessions to the poor and vanished from St. Petersburg for eight years, possibly living with some ascetics and learning from them about the spiritual life.

Blessed Xenia returned to the city clad in one of her husband's old uniforms. She began a life of wandering through the poorer districts of the city, a penitent for her own sins and those of her beloved husband. At first she was taken for a simple-minded beggar. People laughed at and even persecuted her. She bore all her hardships without a murmur, forgiving her tormentors.

Using strange words, Xenia often foretold coming events, including house fires, births, and weddings. People noticed that she never said anything without a reason. Gradually they realized that she was someone other than a mad woman. They began to invite her into their homes, offering warm clothing and alms. She refused all but the smallest of coins, which she then distributed to the poor.

As people began to recognize Xenia's gift of clairvoyance and her meek and humble way of life, they came to see that she was a true fool for Christ's sake. They found signs from God in Xenia's strange behavior. Blessed peace and happiness seemed to settle over any home that received her with sincerity. When she rocked a sick child, the child recovered. Sometimes when visiting she would jump up to leave quickly, saying, "I must hurry; I am needed there." Possessing nothing other than the clothes on her back, she would arrive at the home of a friend and cheerfully announce, "Here is all of me."

Most nights Xenia spent in an open field, prostrating herself in prayer no matter what the weather. It is a miracle that she survived the severe Russian winters. While a new church was being built, workers would arrive in the morning to find bricks moved and mounded where they were needed. After posting a watchman, they discovered that it was Xenia who was helping them in their task. Always willing to help others, the holy fool wandered the streets with a warm, friendly smile on her face, till at last God called His servant to rest.

Today's Holy Fools

Throughout time, the saints have all, in many ways, been fools for Christ in their attempt to follow the gospel mandates. Are there holy fools today? Indeed there are!

In our own times, Mother Teresa's and Dorothy Day's radical gospel-based lifestyles qualified them as fools for Christ. Worldwide, Mother Teresa's Sisters and Brothers of Charity carry on her mission of love and aid to the poor. Similarly, volunteers in a number of houses of the Catholic Worker Movement continue Dorothy Day's radical living of the gospel, with smiles on their faces and love in their hands.

If we follow the gospel mandates, we may also risk being known as fools—fools for Christ.

Angels can fly because they take themselves lightly. Never forget that the devil fell on account of gravity.

G. K. Chesterton

Take courage, I have conquered the world.

JOHN 16:33

The one enthroned in heaven laughs.

PSALM 2:4

FIVE

Laugh at Yourself

Out of gratitude and love for Him, we should desire to be reckoned fools. Laugh and grow strong.

St. Ignatius Loyola

Time and again the saints advise us not to take ourselves too seriously. We must laugh at ourselves. The clown, the buffoon, and the holy fool for God are simply those who first "input" the love of God and then "output" it with contagious joy, laughing and enjoying themselves along the way.

Concepción Cabrera de Armida, a Mexican mother and mystic, showed her ever-present sense of humor in commenting about the difficulties in nursing her first son, who was born in 1885. "He did not want a wet nurse and so had to be fed donkey's milk, evidently the most like mine."

* * *

The insignia of souls united to God are most often gentleness, kindness, and good humor, especially when dealing with the frailties of the human experience. Such holy men and women, having no need for the poses and demands of the world, can move freely as friends of God. St. Crispino of Viterbo was such a friend.

Born in Viterbo, Italy, in 1668, he was consecrated to the

Virgin Mary at the age of five. As a child, Crispino was so spiritually advanced that the villagers affectionately called him *Il Santorello,* "the little saint." Later he was accepted into the Franciscans as a lay brother, assigned to menial tasks. In this capacity he called himself the "little beast of burden of the Capuchins." As he went about his chores without a hat, a passerby asked why he went bareheaded. Crispino confirmed his own nickname: "An ass does not need a hat."[1]

When Pope John Paul II canonized St. Crispino in 1982, he remarked on his joy:

The first aspect of sanctity that I wish to emphasize in St. Crispino is his joy. His affability was known to all the people of Orvieto and to those who approached him, and the peace of God that surpasses all understanding kept his heart and his thoughts (cf. Phil 4:5-7).

Crispino's was a Franciscan joy, sustained by a character rich in ability to communicate and open to poetry, but above all springing from a great love of the Lord and an invincible trust in His providence. "He who loves God with purity of heart," he used to say, "lives happy and dies content."[2]

A Humble Visionary

St. Bernadette Soubirous displayed a wonderful ability to laugh at herself. God chose the fourteen-year-old peasant girl to receive visions and messages from Our Lady at Lourdes, France, in 1858. When she turned sixteen, the local priest arranged for Bernadette to live with the Sisters of Charity and Christian

Instruction of Nevers. He wanted to protect the asthmatic, nearly illiterate girl from the constant interruptions of people who wanted to see her.

Bernadette was just about ready to leave Lourdes for Nevers when she was informed that vendors were selling photographs of her for one franc. Bernadette laughed and responded, "That's much more than I'm worth!"

Bernadette went to live with the sisters, and she eventually joined the order. In the convent some treated her as if she were a saint; others, especially her superiors, dealt with her harshly. She accepted everything, including her chronic illnesses, with humility. She never considered herself someone extraordinary but tried to fit into convent life just like the other sisters.

Bernadette was noted for her sense of humor. At recreation time she told funny stories and sang songs in her native dialect, though she joked that her singing made the other sisters all run away. She had a natural gift of mimicry and provoked much laughter by her imitations of people's mannerisms. Her pithy speech also entertained the sisters. Sick to her stomach after eating roast fowl, she asked for a basin, telling the sister that "my little bird is flying away." She once described an agitated sister as "wriggling like a cut worm."

When the bishop of Rodez was visiting the nuns in Nevers, he passed in front of each sister, allowing each to kiss his ring. He wanted desperately to meet Bernadette, but she decided to avoid him and slipped out a nearby door. Informed later that she had disappointed the bishop and thus had lost forty days' indulgence, Bernadette responded, "Jesus, have mercy on me! There! Now I've gained three hundred days' indulgence!"

When one of the sisters brought up the topic of the apparitions,

Bernadette rhetorically asked her what she did with a broom when she was finished with it: "You put it behind a door, and that is what the Virgin has done with me. While I was useful she used me, and now she has put me behind the door."

The saint knew the source of her joy: "Let the crucifix be not only in my eyes and on my breast but in my heart."

Convent Laughter

Blessed Maria Assunta, the heroic Medical Missionary of Mary, was noted for her smile and serenity. She could turn a clever phrase to make even negative things seem positive. As a novice she was assigned to the care of the animals and other heavy manual labor.

One day a sister met her struggling with a heavy load of hay, dripping with sweat but still smiling. When the sister asked her why she carried so much grass, Sr. Assunta replied gleefully, "My animals are always hungry; they never have enough, but I don't mind. That gives me an extra bath, and it is quite refreshing. All for Jesus, Little Sister."

* * *

The Bavarian Franciscan mystic Blessed Crescentia Hoss was too poor to afford a dowry. She so impressed the Protestant mayor of the town that he begged the sisters to take her in exchange for his past favor of closing a tavern near the convent and giving the property to the nuns. In the convent Crescentia was graced with mystical lights, ecstasies, and visions. She also suffered from diabolical torments. And yet, poetically she prayed for joy and the ability to laugh at herself: "Thou sweet Hand of God givest joy to my heart, and grantest that in pain I play the jester's part."

* * *

The wealthy society belle St. Katherine Drexel chose eternal wealth over the millions of dollars of her personal fortune. The latter she gave for God's poor among the black and Indian peoples of the United States. She considered the distribution of her wealth a privilege rather than a sacrifice.

As a young debutante her sister's death led her to reflect on the meaning of life, wealth, and her future. Undecided about her vocation, she made a list contrasting religious life with life in the world. She then submitted the matter of her vocation to her friend and counselor Bishop O'Connor. She wrote to him that she was in no hurry for his answer. The latest young man to court her had proposed, and she had turned him down. For the time being she felt that her vocation was to be an "old maid."

Years later, as a religious she contracted typhoid fever while visiting the New Mexico missions. When death seemed imminent, she remarked with her usual sense of humor that "as this is certainly not according to my plans, it must be God's will." She recovered fully and was soon back at work, later establishing the Sisters of the Blessed Sacrament.

Laughing on the Run

When the going gets tough, the saints start laughing. The joy that they have internalized in good times remains with them during the worst of times, even unto persecution and death.

The wily and daring Jesuit missionary St. Edmund Campion was one of the first priests to be chosen for the difficult English mission during the time of the persecution of Catholics there. He and his fellow missionaries joked often about the death that awaited them. The night before he left his comfortable scholar's life in Bohemia, a colleague wrote in Latin over the door of his room: "Fr. Edmund Campion, Martyr."

Once in England, Campion's life was spent on the run. The political and religious climate forced him to change his name and location frequently. Though the different disguises he was forced to adopt made him feel ridiculous, he accepted such nuisances matter-of-factly. He wrote to his Jesuit superior June 20, 1580:

> As we want to disguise our persons and to cheat the madness of this world, we are obliged to buy several little things which seem to us altogether absurd. Our journey, these clothes, and four horses which we must buy as soon as we reach England may possibly square with our money; but only with the help of Providence which multiplied the loaves in the wilderness. This indeed is our least difficulty, so let us have done with it.[3]

Edmund frequently read, or was told by people who seemed quite sure of their facts, that Campion, the notorious Jesuit, had been captured. That too must have given him a good laugh.

* * *

Another man on the run was Miguel Gomez Loza, a staunch Catholic lawyer who organized protests against the Mexican government during its persecution of the Church in the 1920s. His spiritual director, Fr. Vicente Maria Camacho, testified that Miguel was jailed no less than fifty-eight times. Loza was incarcerated so often, in fact, that when he married Maria Guadalupe Sanchez Barragan in December 1922, one of his friends told him that the first thing he should buy his wife was a lunch kit so that she could bring him his food in jail.

While in jail Loza remained serene and composed, leading his fellow prisoners in prayer and singing. He wore over his heart an image of the Virgin of Refuge. He often was beaten and several times was at the point of being shot for his faith. He told Fr. Camacho, "It doesn't get me excited."

Joyful in Suffering

Other saints have laughed at their own physical afflictions. The Salesian lay brother Artemide Zatti, who spent himself in loving medical service to the poor of Patagonia, developed cancer of the liver in 1950. As with any liver disease, he began to jaundice and his features puffed out. He told people that he was "ripening like a cantaloupe." The doctors advised him to stay in bed, but he insisted on staying up. "Since my sickness cannot be cured, why should I waste the rest of my life?" he asked.

* * *

St. Vicenta Lopez was never lacking in the humor department. She could even joke about a toothache: "I am doing well, but my molar is giving signs of life. I think that tomorrow we shall condemn it to death." Later she wrote of the marvels of a painless extraction, adding, "The pain came after the extraction of the forty reals [Spanish money] that the doctor took."

* * *

Blessed Mary Theresa Ledochowska as a young countess was stricken with smallpox, which scarred her once beautiful face. She conquered her proud nature and was even able to joke about it when a relative recoiled at the change.

* * *

Saint Bakhita, an African slave girl who grew up to become a Canossian nun, was noted for her cheerfulness and her ability to laugh at herself. During the last four years of her life the once healthy Bakhita fell prey to a number of afflictions, which slowly reduced her to helplessness. Those who came to her sickroom to comfort her soon found their own spirits lifted by the ever-cheerful patient. As she wasted away during her last, painful illness, she said, "I'm all skin and bone—there'll be nothing left for the worms!"

* * *

The Little Flower of Jesus, St. Thérèse of Lisieux, suffered greatly, both physically and spiritually, before her death of tuberculosis at the young age of twenty-four. Ever a realist, in her illness she faced death squarely—and with joyful anticipation. During the last months of her life, she joked with her sister, Mother Agnes of Jesus, saying, "When I think of these words of God: 'My reward is with me, to render to each one according to his works (Rv 22:12),' I tell myself that He will be very much embarrassed in my case. I haven't any works! He will not be able to reward me 'according to my works.' Well, then, He will reward me according to His works."[4]

Earthen Vessels

Ministering to others often highlights one's weaknesses. Many saints show us how to take these frailties in stride.

Fr. Damien, the heroic leper priest of Molokai, was a large, healthy Flemish peasant lad, full of good humor that remained with him his entire life. His professors nicknamed him *le bon gros Damien*—"big, good-natured Damien." His first priestly assignment in the kingdom of Hawaii was in a district so large that it took six weeks to cover by canoe and horseback. Here Damien spent eight years converting the Hawaiians, attending to the Christians, and learning Spanish, Portuguese, and Hawaiian.

Damien's difficulty with the Hawaiian language was a constant source of amusement to the natives. When he could not think of the correct words, he would smile, whip out his handkerchief, and vigorously blow his nose in order to have time to think.

Damien lived for sixteen years at the leper colony on

Molokai, until his own death from leprosy. There he realized the need to lighten the mental load of the lepers, as well as to provide temporal and spiritual help. In order to keep his patients busy, he organized bands and confraternities. The joyous music of the instruments and the prayers and activities of the confraternities brought happiness to the lepers. He enlisted the able-bodied to help construct homes and chapels; this gave them a sense of self-worth and confidence.

* * *

A dedicated layman from the United States, Ira B. "Brother Joseph" Dutton, came to assist Fr. Damien in 1886. Brother Joseph had served in the Union army and had sowed a lot of wild oats; he wanted to help Fr. Damien as an act of personal penance. He stayed on Molokai for forty-four years. In one of his last letters to a friend, written shortly before his death at the age of eighty-eight, Brother Joseph wrote, "I am an old, old relic,... still on duty and happy. Almost ashamed to say how jolly I am. Often I think, we don't know whether our Lord ever laughed; but mine is ready to burst out any moment."

* * *

The saintly Jesuit Miguel Pro, beatified in 1988, could laugh at his sometimes clumsy efforts, even in the tense political climate of Mexico in the 1920s. On more than one occasion he had to deal with babies who had been abandoned on the streets of Mexico City.

I have had six [babies] given to me. The first time it happened, I had no time to send for anyone to fetch the baby, I had to take it away myself. I was imprudent enough to put it, well wrapped up in a big shawl, in a corner of the car. At the first bump the baby gave a leap, and if I had not caught it on the wing, I should have had nothing left to do but take it to the cemetery. I took it into my arms; and I need not tell you in what a state I was when I handed it over to its adopted parents!

* * *

St. Peter Claver, the heroic "slave of the slaves" of Cartagena (now Colombia), met incoming slave ships with food and medicine for the pitiful human cargo. He said, "We must speak to them with our hands before we try to speak to them with our lips." He once said his work was actually a sort of self-indulgence because it ministered to "my enthusiastic and impulsive temperament. If I hadn't something like this to do, I should get into mischief and be a nuisance to people."

Yet he was a nuisance to some. Planters complained that he wasted the slaves' time with his preaching and praying and singing. His detractors even stirred up some of the bishops against him. Fr. groaned, "What sort of man am I that I can't do a little good without causing all this trouble?"

* * *

Blessed Luis Guanella and his friend Pope Pius X liked to joke with one another while carrying out their numerous works of charity. When the pope asked Don Guanella if all his responsibilities did not worry him a great deal, the priest replied, "I worry until midnight, and from then on I let God worry. I even sleep too much. Sometimes when I am in the streetcar and should get off [at one place], I sleep and it takes me to [another place]. And then quietly, and well rested, I return without telling anyone so they will not make fun of me."

Yes, laughing at ourselves is one of the best laughs there is. May God grant us all the humility to do so.

SIX

Enjoy Yourself!

The soul of one who loves God always swims in joy, always keeps holiday, and is always in the mood for singing.

St. John of the Cross

Rejoice in the Lord always. I shall say it again: rejoice! Your kindness should be known to all. The Lord is near. Have no anxiety at all, but in everything, by prayer and petition, with thanksgiving, make your requests known to God. Then the peace of God that surpasses all understanding will guard your hearts and minds in Christ Jesus.

PHILIPPIANS 4:4-7

Today, when life often seems sad and grim, we Christians must learn to enjoy ourselves. There is joy in heaven, but there is also joy on earth as we receive foretastes of joyful eternity in the gifts God gives us daily. The saints have advised us, "Enjoy yourself!"

The love and charity of St. Martin de Porres, the humble Dominican lay brother of Peru, embraced even lower forms of animal life. He excused the problems mice and rats caused in the monastery, saying the poor little things were insufficiently fed. He was overheard ordering the creatures to move from the monastery to the barn, where he promised to provide enough food for them.

We see Martin's love of animals in his recreation. He spent a lot of time working at the friars' farm, and there he played bull-fight with the calves, using his Dominican *cappa* as a *chulo*'s cloak. The calves seemed to enjoy it as much as he did.

Clowning Around

St. Philip Neri, founder of the Oratorians, was known as the "clown-priest" of sixteenth-century Rome. Wherever he went people laughed with him at his hilarious antics. Even before his ordination he had preached in the streets and markets of Rome. His sermons were marked by cheerfulness and good humor, the antithesis of most sermons of his time. Philip held that there was no conflict between spirituality and having a good laugh. He said, "I will have no sad spirits in my house. Cheerful people are more easily led to perfection."

Much of Philip's fame lay in his work as a confessor. He would often give unconventional penances. One gloomy cardinal had to sing the *Miserere* at a wedding. Philip required a young man to go out in the heat of summer wearing a heavy fur coat to cure him of his pride.

On the day of his death in 1595, Philip appeared to be in a radiantly happy mood, bordering on exultation. His doctor gave the opinion that he hadn't looked so well in ten years. He spent a full day hearing confessions and seeing visitors as usual, but before retiring he said, "Last of all, we must die."

About midnight he suffered a hemorrhage so severe that the

fathers were called. He passed to his eternal reward with his hand raised in blessing over the Oratorians in his room.

* * *

Fun-loving as well was Blessed Anuarite Nengapeta, the faithful virgin martyr from Zaire. At recreation time the sisters entertained one another. Anuarite had no talent for singing or dancing, but she had a special knack for making others laugh. At one memorable recreation, costumed in traditional dress, she got up on a table and began a spontaneous display of a traditional war dance. The entire community was reduced to tears of laughter at the sight of the sister-comedienne.

A Playful Saint

Other saints had children as their joyful focus. St. John Bosco worked with boys in the streets of Turin, Italy. He once observed his most famous student, Dominic Savio, rush to the chapel to pray. At recreation time, Bosco observed that the boy declined to play with the other boys. Rosary in hand, young Dominic walked about with a somber expression on his face. For two days he maintained this sober mode. At last his beloved teacher intervened.

"Dominic, are you sick?"

"No," the young boy answered, assuring him that he was quite well and happy.

Then why, asked Don Bosco, had Dominic refused to join in his customary games, and why the sober expression? When

Dominic explained his great desire to be a saint, Don Bosco laughed! Then, praising the boy for his decision, the older man counseled him to be cheerful and not to worry; serving God is the way to true happiness. "Dominic, enjoy yourself as much as you like as long as you keep from sin."

The boy returned to his youthful enthusiasms, following this wise counsel. He was canonized in 1954 as a model for youth.

St. John Bosco knew how to win the most hardened sinner— by showing lovable and persistent kindness and by understanding human weakness. He held a strong belief that good ran through the veins of even the most unpromising characters. He used wit and humor to attract and lead thousands. Even as a boy he entertained people with his acrobatic and juggling feats; as payment for the show he would ask his audience to say a few prayers with him or to attend Mass.

At one house where he boarded as a student, he played so many tricks on his host that the poor man suspected he was in cahoots with the devil and complained to the local canon. The canon called John in for an interview. John politely asked him the time. The hapless canon reached for his pocket watch, but it had disappeared along with his purse. When John returned the items and explained how he had done the tricks, the interview ended with much laughter.

As a student John gathered a group of boys about him. They named themselves "The Merry Company." He was already wise in the knowledge that where there is cheerfulness, there are fewer occasions for sin.

Hundreds of stories attest to Don Bosco's joyful and playful spirit, one of the prime gifts he gave his Salesian Order. It is to his great trust in God that we can ascribe his persistent good humor. He agreed with St. Francis de Sales that "a sad saint is a sorry saint." Instead Don Bosco taught children and religious alike that Christian joy is founded on the possession of a clear conscience, on a proper use of the creatures of this world, and on the joyful freedom of the sons of God.[1]

Don Bosco spoke of and followed vivid "dreams"; as is often the case in the lives of saints, he was misunderstood at times. Some even thought him insane for beginning his works with poor youth and starting construction on magnificent churches when the funds to do so were not at hand.

Two priest friends became so worried about his sanity that they made arrangements for him to enter an asylum. They invited him for a "drive in the country" in order to get him there. When they arrived to pick him up, Don Bosco, with his customary humility, invited them to enter the carriage first. Then, slamming the door, he shouted to the driver, "To the lunatic asylum, quick!" It was only with the greatest difficulty that the two clerics persuaded those at the asylum that the wrong persons had been brought and that they were sane. The entire town roared at the way in which Don Bosco had so neatly turned the tables.

In the early days of Don Bosco's work with boys, poverty and want were familiar companions. Those who visited the converted shed he called the Oratory, however, were forcibly impressed with the joy that goes with innocence and the state of grace. Don Bosco had perfect confidence that any debts he contracted for his work would be paid by Divine Providence, whose banker was Our Lady:

God is in Israel! Let nothing disturb us! If I cannot remove difficulties, I do as the man does who meets an obstacle in his path; he climbs over it or finds a way around. Or, if it would mean useless loss of time, I leave one work and begin another, without losing sight of the first, for the obstacle usually dwindles in time.[2]

Once, while playing happily with his companions, Don Bosco was asked what he would do if an angel told him that in a quarter of an hour he would die and have to appear before the judgment seat of God. The saint promptly replied that he would continue playing, because "I am certain these games are pleasing to God."

Be Happy!

Under the inspiration and tutelage of St. John Bosco, St. Mary Mazzarello, a nearly illiterate peasant girl, began to do a similar work with girls. She infused his spirit of joy into her own congregation, the Daughters of Mary Help of Christians. She, too, knew the power of the precious gift of holy joy.

Counseling a sister afflicted with scruples, Mary told her to go to her room and make a list of all her sins. She cautioned her to write down only real sins, not just the things that existed only in the sister's imagination. Then she instructed her to return and show her the piece of paper, holding it far enough away so that she couldn't read it but could see the amount of sin the girl had.

After some time the girl returned with a blank piece of paper. She began, "I didn't find any real sins, only some little things that..."

Mary interrupted to finish her sentence, "… that don't matter, but fill your head with doubts. Stop wasting precious time on them. Instead, start working and … keep smiling!"[3]

Having learned to write only as an adult, St. Mary Mazzarello's correspondence is not extensive. In form, her letters are simple and conversational with frequent grammar and spelling errors. They are infused, however, with the freshness of her faith and trust in God, her love for God and her neighbor, her humility, disregard for self, and her permanent joy or *allegria*.

The word *allegria* was constantly on her lips as it was in her letters. *Siate allegre, siate allegre* simply translated means "Be happy, keep happy." For the Salesians, however, the words had a deeper meaning, that of being at peace with oneself and one's God. This happiness was not something that came and went but was always there. To keep it one had to practice on a day-to-day, moment-to-moment basis the virtues that were most likely to preserve it—namely charity, obedience, self-sacrifice, purity, and patience.

St. Mary Mazzarello suggested that *allegria* could be acquired by "going about one's daily tasks with simplicity, not seeking satisfaction in people or in the gains of this world but in doing one's duty for the love of God. It also requires one never to be discouraged but to keep on struggling."[4]

This wise and loving foundress sums up her advice: "Laugh and play and dash about as much as you like, only be careful not to say or do anything that would be displeasing to God."

SEVEN

God Loves a Cheerful Giver

He gives most who gives with joy.

Mother Teresa

Each must do as already determined; without sadness or compulsion, for God loves a cheerful giver.

2 CORINTHIANS 9:7

In 1970 the noted British writer Malcolm Muggeridge interviewed Mother Teresa in Calcutta. The result was a film entitled *Something Beautiful for God,* and later a book by the same name, about the work of the Missionaries of Charity. In the preface to the book Muggeridge expresses the hope that it will draw others to help Mother Teresa's work and thereby participate in the love that inspires that work and in the joy that it brings.

After spending a few days with Mother Teresa, Muggeridge remarked to her, "I have been immensely struck by the joyfulness of these Sisters who do what an outsider might think to be almost impossibly difficult and painful tasks."

The humble Albanian foundress replied:

That's the spirit of our society, that total surrender, loving trust, and cheerfulness. We must be able to radiate the joy of

Christ, express it in our actions. If our actions are just useful actions that give no joy to the people, our poor people would never be able to rise up to the call which we want them to hear, the call to come closer to God. We want to make them feel that they are loved. If we went to them with a sad face, we would only make them much more depressed.[1]

One of the four conditions set forth in the Constitutions for the Missionaries of Charity is that postulants must "have common sense and a cheerful disposition." Three virtues Mother Teresa enjoined on her sisters were total surrender, trust, and cheerfulness. Her sisters are known for their smiles and loving nature.

> We can give to the poor everything, even our life; but if we do not give them a smile, we do not give anything.
> *Mother Teresa*

Joyful Service

Once professed as a lay brother of the Holy Cross, for forty years Blessed André Bessette humbly, joyfully, and uncomplainingly washed floors and windows, cleaned lamps, carried firewood, and worked as a porter and messenger. Afterwards he served as a doorkeeper at the order's college in Montreal. He once commented wryly, "When I joined this community the superiors showed me the door, and I remained there for forty years."

Br. André learned the love of God as a child. He knew how to speak of this love with such intensity that he inspired hope in all those who met him. He showed God as a loving Father, gave people common-sense advice, and empathized with those he counseled. These works, along with his warm sense of humor, drew people to him. He said, "You mustn't be sad; it is good to laugh a little." Especially with the poor and the unfortunate the good brother was merry, and his own inner happiness communicated itself to others.

After his work for the day was finished, he visited the sick and the elderly in their homes or in the hospital. He put all of his good nature and good humor into these daily outings. Br. André responded to critics who said he just liked to travel around in a friend's car:

There are some who say that it is for pleasure that I visit the sick, but after a day's work it is far from being a pleasure.... It is not sufficient to give money; one must offer his sympathy and open his heart....

There are homes for the poor filled with men and women who often are abandoned, without relatives or friends. When one is poor, friends are rather scarce. Among these people are found some who had relatives and many friends when they were living in wealth.... It would do healthy men good to visit the sick. This could provide them with good subjects for meditation.[2]

* * *

Although physically disabled, the little foundress of Our Lady's Nurses for the Poor, Eileen O'Connor, had a cheerful nature and a beautiful smile that drew others to her. Indeed, peace and cheerfulness seemed to radiate from Eileen, and Our Lady's Home at Dudley Street became a haven for worried and unhappy people.

Hers was a simple and effective spirituality. Because of her lack of education, her writings are sometimes ungrammatical, but her spirituality shines through them, almost poetically. The simple rules she wrote for Our Lady's Nurses, though not canonical in form, clearly express the spirit she had and passed on to others in her words and her example.

True charity is never idle, for if we wish to be really charitable there is always someone we can make happy or happier, someone we can help a little—make things a little easier for them with our love.

* * *

St. Elizabeth Ann Seton, our first native-born American saint, once wrote, "Every day I ask myself what I do for God in the modest lot that has fallen to me; and I see that I do nothing, only smile, give caresses, exercise patience, write, pray and live, in the expectation of the Lord. O my dear Lord, let thy reign begin."

St. Elizabeth imbued her sisters with a joyful and optimistic charism. Once, in a discussion of their difficulties, one of the younger sisters exclaimed, "My dear sisters, don't grieve so much. Depend upon it, this valley, quiet as it is, will one day give such a roar that all America will hear it."

* * *

Another cheerful giver was Brother Anthony Kowalczyk, O.M.I., a one-armed Polish lay brother currently being considered for beatification. His supporters make no claims of extraordinary supernatural occurrences in his life. Neither did he perform excessive or highly public penances. He merely carried out his daily tasks with outstanding fidelity and love, combined with constant prayer and a gentle sense of humor.

A priest who knew the humble man recalls that Brother Anthony was always happy and wanted those around him to be happy as well: "One day I was working with him and I was in bad humor, grouchy and cranky. Brother Anthony said to me, 'Go away, the Lord doesn't want people who are unhappy working for Him.'"

* * *

Famous for his heroic martyrdom, Blessed Miguel Pro was also prodigious with his charity. By the time of his death, he was supporting over a hundred poor families in Mexico City. He was often seen in the streets of the city with large sacks of provisions on his back. One time he managed to board a bus carrying six live chickens. It mattered nothing to him if the wags he encountered should laugh at him. He would only laugh louder.

Señora Montes de Oca gave Pro lodging in the last days of his life. "He came home on one occasion but there was really nothing to offer him," she said. "The government's people constantly search the house and remove things. He accepted the few biscuits I could give him and went out again laughing,

'They are not enough for me, it is not worth my starting to eat them.' And he took them to some sick people."

Charity ... by Way of the Cross

The wealthy, well-educated Satoko Kitahara spent her life in true Christian charity. She cared for the poor rag pickers and their children who lived at Ants Town in her native Tokyo after World War II. Believing that the poor are best helped when their dignity is respected, she cheerfully joined in the work of selective garbage recycling, long before such efforts became popular. She did much to improve the life and education of the children, arranging many diversions and entertainments to make them happy.

With all the saints, she realized that the way to eternal joy passes by the cross. In August of 1952, shortly before her twenty-third birthday, Satoko was praying and trying to conjure up her normal image of Mary, but all she could see was Our Lady of Sorrows. She wrote:

It would be a precious grace if God asked me to offer myself so that I could make our Mother, Our Lady, smile.... I feel my path to heaven will be a long and painful one. I do not intend to work just for my own eternal salvation, closing my eyes to the people around me. No, I want to offer God many beautiful sacrifices so that I may help others avoid the pains of hell and reach Him in heaven. If my sufferings can help achieve that, what a joy! Then let me embrace suffering!... May the saints in heaven help me discover joy in suffering.... What I must do is ask the Lord for the grace to abandon myself totally to His Divine Providence. Most Sacred Heart of Jesus, I trust in You.[3]

After years of poor health, Satoko died of a nephritis infection, tubercular in origin, in 1958. She died, as she had lived, happily among her beloved poor of Ants Town.

* * *

Venerable Louis Variara wrote to his spiritual daughters, "The cross is sweet because we carry it with Jesus." At the age of nineteen, Brother Louis became the first seminarian to work among the lepers. In keeping with his Salesian spirituality of happiness and activity, Father Variara created a joyful acceptance of the cross among the people of the leper colony of Agua de Dios, Colombia, as well as among the sisters of the unique congregation he founded.

On his arrival at Agua de Dios the colony was dull, monotonous, and seemingly hopeless. The joyful young seminarian began an oratory for the boys, giving them musical instruments and teaching them how to play them. Music and cheerfulness began to enliven the colony.

Some of the girls showed clear signs of a religious vocation, but because they or their parents were lepers, no community would accept them. Fr. Louis thought of a simple plan: he would found an order for them. There they could take advantage of their trying existence by offering themselves to the Lord in an active apostolate among their fellow lepers.

The first seven members of the Daughters of the Sacred Hearts of Jesus and Mary were all leprous women. They formed a community consecrated to suffering and infused with the Salesian spirit of joy. The house of Agua de Dios still keeps its privilege of being open to leprosy-stricken candidates. The sisters dedicate their suffering and distribute their joy in leprosariums and hospitals and among the poorest of the poor in a number of countries.

* * *

Servant of God Mother Marianne Cope brought joy to the despised lepers of Hawaii. When the Hawaiian government asked for help from Catholic religious orders in caring for its afflicted citizens, thirty-six Franciscan Sisters of Syracuse volunteered to go. Mother Marianne and six sisters were selected. Mother Marianne responded as a true daughter of St. Francis to the request to begin a home for "unprotected women and girls" on Molokai; she announced that the sisters "cheerfully will undertake the work."

Throughout her life the Franciscan charism of joy permeated all her actions. She said, "I do not think of reward. I am working for God and do so cheerfully."

After visiting a boys' house, she declared that she was "anxious to help put a little more sunshine into their dreary lives." She revolutionized life on Molokai, bringing cleanliness, pride, and even fun to the colony.

In the words of an old song, "God loves a cheerful giver— give it all you've got!"

EIGHT

Good Cheer Lightens the Load

His way is the way of the cross, which you must shoulder daily, cheerfully, and courageously.

Sr. Miriam Teresa Demjanovich

The recorded lives of the saints display many instances when their sense of humor lightened the load of their daily cares and made even the most difficult situations easier.

The venerable and long-suffering Franciscan Brother Francisco Sanchez took the habit for lay brethren in the Convent of Mexico in 1562. He served many years in the kitchen of that convent, from which he was transferred to the Convent of Puebla. There, during a grave illness, St. Francis appeared to him.

Br. Sanchez had only a shirt, a rosary, and a habit with no cloak—not even a hat. He was a man given to penitence and prayer. He would go to Matins and then, after long spiritual exercises, go cook breakfast for the brothers without returning to his cell.

He maintained his patience; never was his countenance troubled. This was tested at various times, for as the cook he had to bear everything said to him about the food. He would do so as if he did not understand why the brothers were saying

85

it. He would sit down and sing, saying the devil should not take away the worth of the day.

Br. Sanchez left Puebla to return as cook in Mexico, taking on the wardrobe position as well. In one and the other office he was most punctual and charitable; he did as he was asked with dispatch and never spoke an unkind word to anyone. His was a life marked by natural meekness as well as acquired virtues. He died at a holy old age in 1593 in the Convent of Mexico.

Common-Sense Rules

St. Raphaela Mary Porras was the Spanish foundress of the Handmaids of the Sacred Heart. Born into a well-to-do family, as a young girl she was headstrong and vain. One day she was admiring herself in the mirror, rearranging her curls and smiling at how attractive she was. Her priest tutor came up behind her and asked, "Raphaelita, how do you think you will look a quarter hour after your death?"

"That was my conversion," Raphaela said later.

She went on to found the Handmaids and spent over thirty years leading a humble and obedient life, in silent serenity with great charity. She is an example to the universal Church of heroic charity and humility.

Because of her great love and her common sense, Raphaela's community grew rapidly. She used her quick sense of humor to lighten the daily load of her sisters and to guide them. To one sister who was "languishing" Raphaela wrote, "Take good care of yourself; have a good appetite. God does not want His spouses to look as if He fed them on lizards!"

To another sister, in danger of losing her serenity, she wrote, "When you are in a panic, mosquitoes look like elephants." Raphaela made a vigorous plea for cheerful service: "For God's sake, don't let me hear that you have sour faces!"

When she was elected superior general, four advisors were expected to help her govern. Instead, for a variety of reasons, they hindered her work and caused strife. Raphaela believed they were doing as they thought best, and it is a tribute to her that no one outside their small circle suspected the disunity. She wrote in her private retreat notes with her customary humor, "I am nailed to my cross with four painful nails. There is no offence on their part, for like Our Lord's nails they are put there by the Will of the Eternal Father. [I must] live willingly nailed by them."

"How do you think you will look a quarter hour after your death?" Raphaela's tutor had asked. Little had she dreamed that she would be favored with a wondrous expression of peace and happiness after she died. Her body remained incorrupt for thirty years after her death, then followed the natural path of decomposition.

Cheerfulness in Suffering

The young society matron Rose Hawthorne Lathrop watched her friend Emma Lazarus suffer from cancer. Emma's wealth could do little to lighten the load of this dread disease. Yet Rose wondered what happened to the poor who were afflicted with cancer.

She discovered that they were often shunned like lepers. Once they were diagnosed incurable, no hospital would care for them, and many of their families rejected them for fear of contagion. This loving daughter of the famous writer Nathaniel Hawthorne dedicated the rest of her life to nursing the poorest of cancer patients. The religious order she founded, the Dominican Servants of Relief, continues her mission today.

Rose realized that humor and cheerfulness could lighten the load of suffering for her patients. She maintained a happy, cheerful attitude in the homes she founded, often providing unusual treats to cheer up the patients. For one man she bought a radio, for another patient a dog. Once she even acquired a parrot for a patient who was always glum. With this squawking little companion, the man finally cheered up. All of the residents perked up when they experienced the love and tender care of the sisters. Some even remarked that they felt as if they were already in heaven.

* * *

The Poor Clare Sisters witnessed a model of joy in suffering in Blessed Sister Alphonsa, an Indian sister of the Syro-Malabar rite. Even as a child she was known for her joyous observance of all the religious exercises common to this rite. From the time she made her perpetual vows, she said, "it seemed as if a part of the cross of Christ was entrusted to me.... I have a great desire to suffer gladly.... I wish to suffer without betraying even the least sign of suffering."

Sr. Alphonsa willingly accepted all the crosses God was pleased to send her, asking only that she be allowed to suffer gladly. All who knew her say that even when her agony was obviously causing her much suffering, she attempted to smile and only spoke cheerful words. Moments before her death, while she lay serenely on her bed, she smiled and reassured her superior, "Mother, I am in perfect peace."

* * *

The newly beatified stigmatic, Padre Pio of Pietrelcina, reminds us that "the cross doesn't overwhelm; if its weight makes one stagger, its power gives relief." He had a wonderful sense of humor and often made witty remarks using puns or funny vernacular expressions. In the confessional he would sometimes point out a sinner's folly with a quick remark.

Friends teased Padre Pio about his sanctity. Once he alluded to the northern Italians' accusation that southern Italians were "macaroni eaters." In defense of the south he stated, "If they make me a saint, anyone who comes to me seeking a favor will have to bring me first of all a crate of macaroni; for each crate of macaroni, I'll grant a favor!"

Be Cheerful Always!

In many ways Sr. Miriam Teresa Demjanovich seemed to be an ordinary American college student of the 1920s, enjoying to the fullest the happy things of life. However, she was a specially favored soul who received mystical lights. Her writings show that it is God's will for all, no matter what their state in life, to attain sanctity by a close union with Him every day.

Though she was a religious sister, she indulged in the occasional practical joke, although she always stopped short of any unpleasant consequences. Once she carved a perfect banana out of soap and, putting it in a real peel, presented it to a fellow student. She laughingly confessed just as the girl prepared to take a bite; she would not let someone taste the bitterness of her practical joke.

The Sisters of Charity of St. Elizabeth at Convent Station, New Jersey, remember Sr. Miriam as a good and prayerful sister who retained her cheerfulness. She reminds us that, to find the perfect life, we have to keep the ways of the Lord. "His way is the way of the cross, which you must shoulder daily, *cheerfully*, and courageously."

* * *

Br. Elias was a young Trappist at the Abbey of Gethsemani in Kentucky when he died of cancer in 1970. His brothers at the abbey remember him as an exemplary monk whose sense of humor illuminated his life as a modern contemplative. Assigned to the most menial of chores, he was never known to complain. On the contrary, he seemed to radiate peace and joy wherever he went. His cheerfulness and ready smile brought life to those with whom he worked. What he did, he did gladly, lending encouragement to those around him.

Br. Elias' sense of humor endeared him to all the brothers. Once he admonished his spiritual director to slow down. "Look at me," he said. "I'm never in a rush—especially when that bell starts ringing for me to get up at three A.M."

In the final months of his life Elias certainly suffered, but unless directly asked, he made no mention of any pain or discomfort.

* * *

St. Mary Mazzarello, the foundress of the Daughters of Mary Help of Christians, advised her sisters to "be cheerful always; never be sad. Sadness is the mother of tepidity."

On one occasion, Sr. Petronilla, a close friend who had grown up with the saint, mentioned her worry that the rapid growth of the institute might lead to problems, as so many intelligent and well-educated young women were joining. The nearly illiterate saint interrupted her with a stage whisper. "Shh! If they find out how much we don't know, they'll never let us stay."

This beloved saint kept her keen sense of humor until the very day of her death. After receiving the last sacraments she asked, "Father, now that I've got my passport, have I permission to leave?"

Serenity in Trials

Edel Quinn, the Legion of Mary's envoy to Africa, bubbled over with fun. Stricken with tuberculosis, her complete serenity amazed her friends. One of her nurses at the sanatorium said, "She was the nicest girl who ever came here. She made everyone round her happy. She was never in a state of depression and would often laugh till the tears came. Her illness did not appear to weigh on her; she never spoke of it and never complained.

One would have thought she was there on a holiday. Her attitude was one of kindness and helpfulness to all. Anyone in trouble in the sanatorium would at once go to her for consolation."

After something of a recovery, the young Irish girl left her native land for East Africa. She told a friend, "I shall spend nine years in Africa and die there." A few days before departure she told one of the Legionaries, "Pray for me, and keep joking as much as you can so that I shall not break down."

* * *

As a child Countess Annetta Bentivoglio was so happy and mischievous that her mother once remarked, "You are something very different from a saint!" Although she eventually entered a saintly path, she was always known for being high-spirited and full of fun.

Late in life she recalled a youthful trip with St. Madeleine Sophie Barat. At one inn there was only a single bed for the two. Annetta said, "And so I slept with a saint, and I kicked the saint!" She and her sister became Poor Clare nuns. Annetta took the name of Mother Magdalen.

In 1875 Mother Magdalen and her sister answered an appeal of Pope Pius IX to go to America to form a contemplative monastery in the mission territory there. In his farewell address the pope asked them to "be a silent sermon accompanied by prayer and union with God, to make known to many that true happiness is not to be found in things temporal and material."

The sisters eventually founded their monastery in Omaha.

Difficulties arose because of the language barrier. During one particularly upsetting trial, which Venerable Mother Magdalen accepted without bitterness, her sister said, "They must think we are fools. We are under the most fearful accusations, and here you are laughing!"

"I cannot help it," she replied. "All my life I have asked God for crosses, and now that He has sent them, why should I not be glad?"

Even when life in the cloister became most difficult, Mother Magdalen managed to retain her sense of humor. In one letter she wrote, "We are without shoes and stockings; we shall see if we can stand it. It is certain that on the one hand we do not want to pamper anyone, but on the other hand we do not want to kill anyone."

* * *

Another holy woman who began life with a mischievous reputation was Maria de la Luz Camacho. One favorite trick was to take a coin attached to a thread and drop it from the window just as an unsuspecting person passed by. The person would of course stoop to pick up the coin when, "presto," it would disappear.

At the time of Maria's birth, her native Mexico was in a relatively peaceful period. By her teenage years, however, the churches were closed and the faith was kept alive only by the sturdiness of Mexican Catholics. "The Great Friend," as the Mexican people called the Divine Presence in the sacrament of the altar, came to the people in their homes; there was only one priest for every four thousand people.

At fifteen Maria trained as a catechist. She established in her home a center where, on Saturday nights, about eighty children came to hear the truths of the Catholic faith. Although Maria had the philosophical grasp of an adult, she entertained her young charges with jokes and marionettes. Maria also wrote and staged a number of plays for the people of her town of Coyoacan.

Like all of us, Maria sometimes suffered from hurt feelings and interior trials. She told her confessor, "Do good and let people talk. When one can bear the pain alone, why make others suffer?"

This vivacious and outgoing young woman was shot on the steps of her parish church, defending it against a group of young communists known as the Red Shirts. She was the first martyr of Catholic Action of Mexico, and her cause for beatification has begun.

It is natural that in our daily lives we should at times experience pain, suffering, sadness, boredom, and other ills. The saints show us that humor can lighten the day and give us the peace we seek.

NINE

Out of the Mouths of Babes

Jesus said, "Let the children come to me, and do not prevent them, for the kingdom of heaven belongs to such as these."
MATTHEW 19:14

Children receive the love of God in a way befitting them. The Church numbers children of varying ages, from all over the world, among its saints and saints-to-be. In addition, many saints who grew to adulthood first experienced the love of God at a very young age.

Children also have their own apostolic work to do. In their own way, they can be true living witnesses to Christ among their companions.

Vatican II, *Decree on the Apostolate of the Lait III, 2*

The psalmist reminds us that truth can come "out of the mouths of babes (see Ps 8:2)." Young followers of Christ offer us wise counsel about the power of joy and a smile.

At the age of ten St. Thérèse of Lisieux learned about the power of a smile from no less a teacher than Our Blessed Mother. Thérèse was suffering from a strange illness that baffled her doctors. Indeed, they feared she might not survive. Thérèse tells what happened on May 13, 1883, when she looked at the family's statue of Our Lady, which had been moved into her sickroom.

> All of a sudden the Blessed Virgin appeared beautiful to me, so beautiful that never had I seen anything so attractive; her face was suffused with an ineffable benevolence and tenderness, but what penetrated to the very depths of my soul was the ravishing smile of the Blessed Virgin. At that instant all my pain disappeared and two large tears glistened on my eyelashes and flowed down my cheeks silently, but they were tears of unmixed joy. Ah! I thought, the Blessed Virgin smiled at me, how happy I am.[1]

At that moment Thérèse was cured. During the process of beatification for this Little Flower of Lisieux, her sister Marie (Sr. Marie of the Sacred Heart) testified of the healing: "I saw Thérèse as in an ecstasy, and I understood that she was looking not at the statue but at the Blessed Virgin."

Youthful Courage

Many child saints experienced tremendous suffering with grace and confidence. Montserrat Grases, a Spanish girl being considered for beatification, died of bone cancer at the age of eighteen. Before her death she said to her father, "We are the happiest family in Barcelona. When I die, I don't want anyone to be sad, there has to be joy."

The course of her cancer ran normally, painfully, and rapidly. "Montsie," as she was known to her friends, accepted her suffering heroically and even made light of it. After her death her pastor said, "In a case like this, instead of being sad and offering sympathy, you have to intone the Alleluia."

* * *

Another young Spanish candidate for the honors of the altar is Santos Franco Sanchez, who died of meningitis in 1954 at the tender age of eleven. He too counseled his family against sadness: "Soon I am going to heaven; I have very little time left. I will not forget you. I love you very much. Don't cry, because I am happy. What do sufferings matter? Heaven! How beautiful, God and the Blessed Mother are there."

* * *

Alexia Gonzalez-Barros died of cancer in 1985 at the age of fourteen. In the hospital toward the end of her illness, a large metal device was fitted to her head and neck with screws, and she was given a medication that turned her mouth purple. She turned to a visitor and said, "First they made me look like Frankenstein; now I look more like Dracula!" In spite of the horror of Alexia's condition, the friend had no option but to laugh at the young teen's comment.

Earlier Alexia's mother had brought her a woolen cap to

keep her head warm, since all her hair had fallen out from chemotherapy. Alexia asked her mother to embroider "I am bald" on the cap.

To visitors Alexia always presented a cheerful demeanor, turning the conversation to them and away from her own problems. One of her doctors brought his students to see her, telling them, "I want you to see how it is to be joyful, despite pain and suffering."

Alexia accepted her fatal illness, kept her sense of humor, offered her suffering for others, and faithfully lived her motto and constant prayer, "Jesus, may I always do what You want." Joy was the hallmark of her brief life.

* * *

Annie Zelikova was seventeen years old when she died of tuberculosis in 1941. The entrance of her cause for beatification in Rome confirms this Czech girl's reputation for holiness. A third order Carmelite, Annie was known as an "apostle of the smile."

On the final night of her life, lying on a bed of pain, Annie told a visitor, "I must smile to my last breath. Ah, all I can give God now are my heartbeats and my smile. Nothing is left to me except love and trust."

A short time later Annie's mother realized that the end was near. She kept vigil with her teenage daughter, praying the rosary as the last vestiges of life slipped away. Just before dawn, in the age-old custom of the Moravian people, she placed the Candlemas candle in her daughter's hands, supporting both Annie and the candle.

Annie's beloved Jesus had granted all that she asked of Him, to do only with her as he willed. Surely He would not deny her last wish—to die with a smile. Her face broke into one of her beautiful smiles, and slowly she spoke, "How beautiful ... it all is.... I wouldn't ... trade places... with anyone. My heart ... is beating ... for Jesus. I love Him so much."

Her last audible statement was a weak but definitive "I trust." As the Angelus began to chime, Annie's head fell back upon her pillow. The smiling eyes, which in life sought only to give pleasure to Jesus and to gain souls, fluttered gently and closed.

Joy at Fatima

The call for joy from our youngest saints sounds again and again.

Although the message of Fatima was a call to repentance and penance, the young seers Jacinta and Francisco Marto were no strangers to joy. These two illiterate shepherd children are the youngest nonmartyrs ever beatified. They were not acclaimed among the blessed because of their visions of Our Lady but for their virtues, which proved heroic even in their short lives.

Francisco had a naturally calm temperament and was extremely good-natured. Observers testified that he was radiant with joy on receiving his First Holy Communion the day before his death. His sister Jacinta was of a happy and outgoing nature, sweet and affectionate. After the encounter with the Blessed Mother she became more solemn, constantly making sacrifices for souls as the Lady had requested. These were childish sacrifices, but sacrifices nonetheless.

Jacinta loved to dance. On one occasion the children were being held in jail by government authorities, who were trying to terrorize them into recanting their account of the visions. One of the prisoners sought to divert the children's attention from their difficult plight by playing a concertina. Jacinta began to dance with a poor thief. He found her so small that he picked her up and went on dancing with her in his arms! Later she told Lucia, the third and sole surviving seer, that she was going to give up her pleasure in dancing as a sacrifice for Our Lord.

Before Jacinta died, Our Lady let her know that the girl would die alone in the hospital. Having visited her, Lucia said, "I found Jacinta as joyful as ever, glad to suffer for the love of our Good God and of the Immaculate Heart of Mary, for sinners and the Holy Father."

The mother of Jacinta was notably grieved at seeing her daughter so ill. Jacinta would say, "Don't worry, Mother. I'm going to heaven, and there I'll be praying so much for you," or simply, "Don't cry. I'm all right."

A Life Short and Full

The United States may one day claim its own child saint: Charlene Richard, a little Cajun girl. She lived a simple life in her rural home at Richard, Louisiana, in the diocese of Lafayette. The people of Charlene's small community live simply but are strong in faith. After her death they began to ask Charlene's intercession for help over the rough spots in their lives. In return, she seemed to shower favors on those who asked in humble faith.

Happiness is in the nature of children, and Charlene was no exception. She was an avid sports enthusiast, playing on her school softball and basketball teams. She baked cookies, rode horses, and enjoyed being with her friends. With typical Cajun humor, Charlene loved to "pick at" her friends and relatives. One summer evening she spied her Aunt Ora, who was spending the night, dressed for bed in a nylon gown that had developed a number of "wear and tear" holes. Charlene looked up and slyly said in French, "Oh, Honey, that's the gown!"

Charlene's family was not wealthy, and their home, though clean and comfortable, did not have many modern conveniences. One of Charlene's brothers says that the children never knew they were poor because they had so much fun.

In 1959 Charlene was diagnosed with acute lymphatic leukemia. She died just thirteen days after the diagnosis. During her last few days on earth, Charlene suffered terribly, although the doctors did what little they could to make her comfortable.

Sr. M. Theresita Crowley, the pediatric supervisor at the time Charlene entered Our Lady of Lourdes hospital in Lafayette, remembers Charlene as a pious little girl:

Charlene suffered a great deal; it's the nature of the disease. The pain is awful, and there is almost constant bleeding and hemorrhage. But I remember her as a cheerful patient. She never complained.... Of all the beautiful, sick children I have tended to in my career as a nurse, Charlene stands out in a very special way. I learned a lot from Charlene, especially from her willingness to accept everything. Her life was full in a short span.[2]

Embracing the Crown of Martyrdom

Joy and happiness are mentioned often in the lives of the child martyrs. Witnesses testified that Kizito, the youngest of the Ugandan martyrs, went to his death laughing and singing as if the death march were a game.

St. Peter Yu was martyred at age thirteen in Korea. In spite of the cruelest of tortures, witnesses say that his love of God seemed to change his face and ridicule the torturing adults; he remained happy and smiling, full of a miraculous courage. Truly even the youngest of our saints can inspire us to joy, both by their words and by their actions.

The sisters who taught Blessed Laura Vicuna testified that she seemed to build a joyful spirit of piety in her fellow students. At the tender age of twelve, Laura was beaten to death on a street in Argentina by her mother's illicit lover. As she lay dying, she told her mother, "Mama, I'm dying, but I'm happy to offer my life for you. I asked Our Lord for this."

Through the witness of her courageous daughter, Laura's mother returned to the practice of the faith. The young martyr of purity was beatified in 1988.

Truly, youth can be wise teachers. And as these prove, they have much to teach us about true joy!

TEN

Sometimes It's All Right to Cry

If you love me, do not weep.... Why do you who saw me and loved me in the land of shadows, why do you think you will not see me and love me again in the land of unchanging realities?

St. Monica

Jesus wept.

JOHN 11:35

All the saints were human beings and, as such, subject to the normal range of human feelings. Although filled with the love of God and the joy of the Resurrection, they were not unmoved by the sadness and affections of life. Indeed, some of our "happiest" saints displayed profound grief at the loss of a loved one.

Bidding Mama Good-Bye

When Don Bosco, that perennial promoter of youthful cheerfulness, began his work with the street boys of Turin, his mother Margaret came to help him. Loved and accepted by the boys for her motherly heart, she, too, walked the path of sanctity.

After eight years, the elderly, faith-filled woman was ready to go home. "Mama Margaret's" work was done, and she lay dying of pneumonia. The news spread, and the boys thronged the chapel. As she lay dying, she reminded her son that she had once helped him receive the Last Sacraments when there was fear that he was dying, and that now he must assist her.

Sorrowfully, Don Bosco nodded assent. She received the sacraments calmly, recognizing the full seriousness of her condition. She gave both her sons farewell advice, reminding Don Bosco to tell the boys—who were uppermost in her mind—of her love. She promised that if, by the mercy of God, she were to go to heaven, she would pray unceasingly for the Oratory her son had established.

That last earthly night, her sons watched at the bedside. Joseph was calm, but John's grief was unconcealed. Noticing this, she beckoned him near and whispered, "Johnnie dear, God knows how much I have loved you in the course of my life. I hope to be able to love you more in heaven." Her tears overcame her, and Don Bosco broke down, too.

Then, courageously, Margaret sent John away. "Go, my dearest John, go away because you make me sorrowful to see you so afflicted. Besides, you suffer more seeing me in these last moments. Good-bye, John. Remember that this life consists in suffering. True pleasures will be found in heaven. Go into your room and pray for me."

He left for a time and then returned. She noticed him at once and motioned him to depart so as not to witness her agony. When he did not leave she said, "John, you are not able to endure this sight." Don Bosco, weeping, protested in a broken voice, "Mother, it is not the part of an affectionate son to abandon you at this time."

After a few moments' silence, Margaret spoke with difficulty, "Johnnie, Johnnie, I ask you for a favor and it is the last that I ask of you. My suffering is doubled seeing you suffer. I have enough help here." (Others in the room included some priests, her son Joseph, and her sister.) "You go away and pray for me. I ask nothing else. Good-bye, Johnnie."

The obedient son of the saintly mother left her chamber to pray and cry in his room. Later, when the weeping boys crowded around him, he was able to compose himself and say, "We have lost our mother, but I am sure that she will help us from her place in paradise. She was a saint."

A Time for Tears

Blessed Miguel Pro, the heroic Mexican martyr, also suffered the grief of losing a godly mother. The Jesuits were expelled from Mexico when Miguel was still a novice. Forced to leave his beloved homeland and family, Miguel finished his novitiate and other studies in California, Spain, Nicaragua, and Belgium. In addition to his homesickness, severe stomach problems beleaguered him.

Miguel was known for his happy, upbeat nature. One of his fellow students noticed that whenever he received a letter from home with bad news, he would play one of his most outrageous tricks. Thus Miguel concealed his longing for his family. He often dealt with the ever-increasing pains in his stomach by telling a joke. This gave him an excuse to hold his sides and make funny faces to cover a grimace of pain.

In time Miguel developed insomnia and was unable to eat. His superiors noticed the dramatic change in his physical appearance. They sent him for medical treatment, including an operation for bleeding ulcers.

Shortly after his surgery Miguel received the news of his mother's death. At first stunned, he spent the night clutching his crucifix and weeping for the one who had been closer to his heart than any other human being. He mentioned to his fellow religious his intuition that his saintly mother was already in heaven: "This morning I wished to say Mass for the peace of her soul, but I could not pray for her; from this I'm certain she is already in heaven."

To a friend he confided:

Sorrow is not contrary to perfect conformity to the will of God, so I still mourn.... She is in heaven; from thence she sees me, blesses me, and takes care of me. However, that does not stop her orphan children from shedding torrents of tears, nor from feeling in their souls a sorrow that only God can measure.[1]

This kind of profound sorrow so deeply touched Concepción Cabrera de Armida during the first days of her widowhood that the doctors feared she would die. The thought of her husband was with her constantly, and the sound of her children crying over their father pierced her soul. Nor did her sorrows end with the death of her husband. Three of her eight children died in her arms.

To one son who later became a Jesuit priest she wrote, "Become a saint. Life is too short to stop along the road. No matter what path we take to seek God, it always passes by the cross.... Love it, for it is the main instrument of our salvation."

Although the saints suffered and cried, at the last their tears were wiped away by that love that is eternal joy. Concepción, usually known as "Conchita," is today considered a model for wives and mothers everywhere. The most prolific writer of any of the mystics of our time, her spiritual diary fills sixty-six volumes. Smiling and cheerful, she left the legacy of a real, warm, loving, and faithful woman who constantly displayed all the virtues proper to her state of life. In spite of her hidden penances and mortifications, her disappointments and hurts, and a chronic illness, she always followed the down-to-earth advice she gave her daughter: "Whatever God asks you to do, do it with a smile."

Confessions of a Saint

"Thou hast made us, O Lord, for Thee, and our heart is unquiet until it rests in Thee." With these words St. Augustine began his *Confessions,* the most honest and impressive autobiography in the literature of the world.

Born in 354 in what is today known as Algeria, Augustine had an ambitious, unbridled youth. He had no peace of soul and vainly sought it in the heretical sect of the Manicheans. He traveled to Italy, where he taught rhetoric. In 386, by the grace of God, the tearful prayers of his holy mother St. Monica, and the influence of saintly friends, he was converted and baptized along with his son by St. Ambrose. Augustine devoted himself entirely to God. He was ordained a priest in 391 and in 394 was made bishop of Hippo. Today he is known as one of the greatest of the Doctors of the Church.

After his baptism Augustine and his mother set out to return to Africa. At Ostia they had a moving conversation on the everlasting life of the blessed. Five days later Monica fell ill and died. After her death, Augustine seemed to hear her soul speaking to him:

If you love me, do not weep. If you only knew the gift of God and what heaven is! If only you could hear the angels' song from where you are, and see me among them! If you could only see before your eyes the eternal fields with their horizons and the new paths in which I walk! If only you could contemplate for one moment the beauty that I see, beauty before which all others fail and fade! Why do you who saw me and loved me in the land of shadows, why do you think you will not see me and love me again in the land of unchanging realities? Believe me, when death breaks your chains as it has broken mine, when, on the day chosen by God your soul reaches heaven where I have preceded you, then you will see her who loved and still loves you. You will find her heart the same, her tenderness even purer than before. God forbid that on entering a happier life, I should become less loving, unfaithful to the memories and real joys of my other life. You will see me again transfigured in ecstasy and happiness, no longer waiting for death, but ever hand in hand with you, walking in the new paths of light and life, slaking my thirst to the full at the feet of God from a fount of which one never tires, and which you will come to share with me. Wipe away your tears, and if you love me truly, weep no more.[2]

ELEVEN

The Joy of the Martyrs

Let us rush with joy and trepidation to the noble contest and with no fear of our enemies. If they see our spirits cowering and trembling, they will make a more vigorous attack against us. They hesitate to grapple with a bold fighter.

St. John Climacus

Though St. John Climacus was not a martyr, these words aptly convey the eagerness with which many of the saints aspired to the martyr's crown. Entire volumes could be filled in recounting the joy expressed by the Christian martyrs down through the centuries. Just as the blood of the martyrs is the seed of the Church, the joy of the martyrs is a contagious one.

* * *

Fr. Peter Dumoulin Borie, a French priest, was one of the 117 martyrs of Vietnam canonized in 1988. His captors beat him with bamboo sticks and rubbed salt in his wounds in order to get him to tell them who had sheltered him. When an official taunted him and asked, "Does it hurt?" Fr. Borie replied, "I'm made of skin and bone like other men; of course it hurts. But I was happy before and I am happy now." His spirit could not be broken.

109

The official in charge of his execution expressed his regret that the priest had to die. Father Borie told him, "To show how grateful I am for the privilege of dying thus, let me prostrate before the man who has brought it about." The officer would not allow it and burst into tears.

Heaven in View

The joy and even humor Christian martyrs have displayed in the face of torture and execution do not indicate a desire to escape the sorrows of this world. Rather they manifest the saints' supreme faith and happiness to be entering another, better world.

Simply to be a Christian in the early days of the Church implied that one was in daily danger of dying for the faith. Alban Butler, perhaps the greatest of hagiographers, records several instances of those who were eager to follow Christ's path and attain the crown of martyrdom.

It is said that when St. Peter was on his way out of Rome to escape martyrdom, he met Jesus on the road going the other way. Peter asked him, "Where are you going, Lord?"

Christ replied, "Follow me. I am going to Rome to be crucified again."

Tradition tells us that St. Peter asked to be crucified upside down. For "as Christ came down to earth from heaven, He was crucified with His feet pointing downward; but since I am being summoned from earth to heaven, it is fitting that my head should be down and my feet pointing upward."

When the Roman soldiers arrived to arrest the gentle, humble bishop of Antioch, St. Ignatius (d. 107), he "joyfully submitted his limbs to the fetters." Informed that he would be fed to the lions, the saint replied, "I have joy of the beasts that are prepared for me."

St. Polycarp (d. 155), bishop of Smyrna, was burned at the stake and pierced with a spear. A witness observed that "he appeared in a transport of joy and confidence, and his countenance shone with a certain heavenly grace."

St. Perpetua (d. 203) wrote that after the judge "condemned us to the wild beasts, we returned joyfully to our prison."

When St. Lawrence (d. 258), a deacon in the Roman church, heard he was to be arrested, he "was full of joy ... and gave everything to the poor." He was stripped, bound, and placed on a large gridiron above burning coals. After suffering a long time, he turned to the judge and said with a cheerful smile, "Let my body be turned; one side is broiled enough." Later he said, "It is cooked enough. You may eat," and then he died.

St. Agnes was condemned to beheading in the third or fourth century. St. Ambrose wrote, "Agnes, filled with joy on hearing this sentence, went to the place of execution more cheerfully than others go to their wedding."

The persecutions under the Emperor Diocletian in the fourth century were especially cruel. Once, in Rome, a comedy was presented to entertain the pagan emperor. One of the comedians, a pagan named Genesius (d. c. 300), lay down on the stage, pretending to be ill and crying out, "I am resolved to die a Christian." Actors playing a priest and an exorcist were called, and the comedian told them, "I desire to be born again and to be delivered from my sins." The actors went through a mock baptismal ceremony, and then those actors playing soldiers seized Genesius and presented him to the emperor.

While acting, however, Genesius had been suddenly converted. He told Diocletian very seriously, "Hear, O Emperor, I am truly a Christian," then urged the audience to accept Jesus Christ as their Lord and obtain forgiveness of their sins. Diocletian at first supposed Genesius still to be acting. When the comedian continued to insist that he was a Christian, the emperor became enraged and ordered him beaten, tortured, and beheaded.

Witty to the End

St. Thomas More (d. 1535) has often been acclaimed as the wittiest of Christian martyrs. His first wife bore him four children, and the family lived in happiness and much good humor. After the death of his first wife, More married a widow who helped him raise his children. His only complaint against her was that she did not appreciate his jokes.

More became Lord Chancellor of England and counselor to King Henry VIII. When the king put away his queen to marry Anne Boleyn, More resigned his position and withdrew from public life. Reduced to poverty, he called his family together to explain their difficult situation, telling them they would have to go begging and singing and "so still keep company and be merry together."

More was imprisoned in the Tower of London for his protest of the king's marriage. At his trial he told his judges that although they had condemned him, he would pray that "yet hereafter in heaven [we may] merrily all meet together to everlasting salvation." In his last letter, written to his beloved daughter Margaret, he wrote, "Farewell, my dear child, and pray for me, and I shall for you and all your friends that we may meet merrily in heaven."

Jesting even at the point of death, he told his executioner, "I pray thee, see me safe up, and for my coming down let me shift for myself." To the end he called himself "the King's good servant, but God's first." As he laid his head on the block, he made his final and most famous wisecrack. Carefully pushing aside his luxuriant beard, he murmured, "This hath not offended the King."

* * *

Another Catholic layperson who lived and died valiantly in the English persecution was St. Margaret Clitherow (d. 1586). Described as "full of wit, very merry, and loved by everyone," she called prison "a most happy and profitable school," for there she found the joy of spiritual growth and also learned to read and write.

Indeed, Margaret was imprisoned several times. She was eventually arrested for harboring and maintaining a priest. With a laugh she told the messenger who gave her this warrant, "I wish I had something to give you for this good news. Wait, take this fig—I have nothing better."

A contemporary wrote, "Her high spirits never forsook her, and when two days later she was joined by Mrs. Ann Tesh, the two friends joked and laughed together." Looking out a window at other Catholic prisoners, she told Ann that she was going to make them laugh, too. Then she held up her fingers in the form of a gallows.

The judge was unwilling to sentence the pretty thirty-year-old and begged her to enter a plea. She would not, so she was finally pronounced "mute of malice" and was condemned to be pressed to death.

Although Margaret looked forward to a martyr's crown, she did not trust her own strength and so spent her remaining days fasting and praying. Her last night she wistfully remarked to her cellmate that she wished she had a friend to keep her company, to encourage her, and to pray with her. The woman, a Protestant imprisoned as a debtor, spent part of the night praying with her. Margaret walked to her execution barefoot, with ribbons in her hair. She had sent her shoes to her daughter as a sign for her to follow in her mother's footsteps.

The crowd marveled at the radiance of Margaret's face; she looked as happy as a bride going to her wedding. The sentence dictated that Margaret be stripped naked for the execution, but she was spared this humiliation and allowed to wear a simple linen dress that she had made for the occasion. It had strings sewn to the sleeves so the executioner could tie her hands to the posts before placing a heavy door on her body. She was crushed to death in fifteen minutes.

Viva Cristo Rey!

The 1920s were a grim time for the Church in Mexico. In 1926 the Mexican government deported or imprisoned bishops, priests, and religious. New laws forbade the celebration of the sacraments. When the bishops closed the churches in protest against such measures, they instructed the faithful to make their homes and hearts centers of worship for Christ the King. The Catholic Church in Mexico went underground.

Twenty-five Mexicans martyred in those years were canonized in May 2000, and there are a number of other causes for beatification entered in Rome. One of the best known martyrs from this time is the high-spirited Blessed Miguel Pro.

As a child Miguel was full of energy and joy. His penchant for practical jokes found an outlet in his large and loving family and among many friends, who learned to respond in kind. Along with his happy nature, Miguel had a deep spirituality and was devoted to Christ the King and Our Lady of Guadalupe. He became convinced of his call to the priesthood and joined the Jesuits in 1911.

The Jesuits were exiled from Mexico in 1914, so Miguel studied abroad and was ordained in Belgium in 1925. He returned to Mexico to minister secretly. Within twenty-three days of his arrival, the order suppressing all public worship was issued. Priests were subject to arrest and prosecution.

Fr. Pro's life story during this time reads like the best of espionage novels. His letters are filled with cheerful descriptions of his daily clandestine works. In addition to celebrating Mass and administering the sacraments in secret, he collected and distributed food and supplies to the poor of the city. He barely escaped capture on several occasions.

Once he was riding in a taxi when he realized the police were following him. As the taxi rounded a corner, Fr. Pro ordered the driver to slow down. He rolled out of the car, stood up, lit a cigar, and approached an attractive and very startled young woman. Quickly whispering, "Help me, I am a priest," he grabbed the woman's arm. When the police caught up, they saw only a seemingly love-struck couple strolling down the street.

In order to carry out his ministry, the valiant young priest adopted a number of disguises, including those of a chauffeur, garage mechanic, farm laborer, playboy, and policeman. He might show up in the middle of the night dressed as a beggar in order to baptize an infant. Or, dressed as a policeman, he might slip into police headquarters to hear confession and give viaticum to Catholic prisoners awaiting execution. His messages to underground Catholics and to his superiors were coded and signed "Cocol," to remind the people not only of the type of sweet bread he favored but also of the Sweet Bread of the sacrament that he brought them.

One of Miguel's ideas resulted in a great joke on the government. On December 4, 1926, the resistance released six hundred balloons in the area over Mexico City. The balloons soon began to drop their cargo of brightly colored religious leaflets. The president was furious at being made to look a fool in his own city and demanded reprisals.

In November 1927 the heroic priest was finally caught and condemned with no due process or trial. The first to be led out for execution that day, Miguel blessed and forgave the firing squad. He knelt for a brief prayer and, rejecting the traditional blindfold, stretched his arms out in the form of a cross and declared, *"Viva Cristo Rey!"*—"Long Live Christ the King!"—as the gunmen shot him down.

The inscription placed over the chapel that guards Pro's remains in Mexico City recognizes joy as his hallmark: "In this chapel is venerated the Mexican Fr. Miguel Agustin Pro, S.J., 1927, model of happiness and fulfillment of duty."

Ready to Join the King

Another of the heroic Mexican martyrs of the 1920s was Luis Magana Servin. On the morning of February 9, 1928, federal soldiers came to the Magana home to arrest Luis, who was suspected of aiding the *Cristeros* (the Catholics in armed rebellion). Not finding him at home, they took his younger brother Delfino, telling the family that if Luis didn't turn himself in that day, they would shoot their prisoner.

When Luis returned home for lunch, he found his wife and parents in tears. They told him what had happened, and with his usual serenity he said, "Be calm. I will speak with General Martinez to find out what is going on, and I promise you to bring Delfino here. At the most, they will take me to Guadalajara, where they are taking everyone."

Luis bathed, shaved, and dressed in a new suit. He ate lunch tranquilly with his family. Then he knelt in front of his parents and asked their blessing. He hugged them all, kissed his young son, and left.

A friend saw him walking and asked where he was going so dressed up. On learning what was going on, he told Luis, "Don't go, they will shoot you!" Luis, opening his arms and looking at the sky, replied, "What happiness! Within an hour I will be in the arms of God."

Luis made his way to the military office and was taken to the general, who demanded, "Who are you?"

"My General, I am Luis Magana, whom you are looking for," he said without a tremble, looking the general in the eye. "The one you have detained is my brother, and he hasn't done anything. Now that you have me, turn him loose."

General Martinez saw before him a valiant man, dressed as for a fiesta, calm and serene as if he were going to be given an award. Rising from his seat, he had a few words with his lieutenant, then said to Luis, "Well, young man, we are going to see if in truth you are as valiant as you seem." He ordered the guards, "Let the other go, and shoot this one immediately in the patio of the church."

It was nearly four in the afternoon, and the streets were almost deserted. The firing squad of eight soldiers left with Luis and with Pancho Muerte, who had also been arrested. Crossing the town plaza, the group entered the atrium of the church. Luis refused the traditional blindfold and asked to say a few words. Two witnesses in nearby hiding places have given testimony to what happened.

Luis said, "I am neither a *Cristero* nor a rebel. But if you accuse me of being a Christian, that I am. Soldiers that are going to shoot me, I want to tell you that from this moment I pardon you and I promise you that on arriving in the presence of God, you are the first ones I will intercede for. *Viva Cristo Rey! Viva Santa Maria de Guadalupe!*"

The sounds of the bullets carried throughout the still town on that sad afternoon. The Magana family, on hearing the sounds, knew in their hearts that it was their own martyr who had been executed—a martyr sad to leave his family but joyful to join his King.[1]

Modern Martyrs

Blessed Titus Brandsma was a fiery Dutch priest and journalist who stood up to the Nazis in the Dutch Catholic press. This started him on a road that was to end at Dachau.

In his position as national spiritual advisor to Catholic journalists, Fr. Brandsma delivered a mandate that any publication printing Nazi propaganda could not claim to be Catholic. The Nazis began to call him "that dangerous little friar."

Fr. Brandsma knew he would be arrested. When someone reminded him of his danger he said, "Well, now I am going to get what has so seldom been my lot, and what I have always wanted—a cell of my own. At last I shall be a real Carmelite."

From prison he wrote to his brother priests, "I don't need to weep or sigh. I even sing now and then, but of course not too loud." His fellow Carmelites laughed at this, because sometimes in chapel Titus had forgotten himself and roared out the hymns in enjoyment.

At the prison in Amersfoort the guards were cruel. Titus urged the other prisoners to pray for them, but they felt it was a difficult request. He lightened his request with his customary humor: "Well, you don't need to pray for them all day long; God is quite pleased with a single prayer!"

Pope John Paul II has called ours an age of martyrs. During the twentieth century up to our present day, thousands upon thousands of Christians have suffered martyrdom for the faith. One of them, Archbishop Oscar Romero of San Salvador, beautifully expressed the Christian's mandate to live joyfully in every circumstance:

It is wrong to be sad. Christians cannot be pessimists. Christians must always nourish in their hearts the fullness of joy. Try it, brothers and sisters; I have tried it many times and in the darkest moments, when slander and persecution were at their worst: to unite myself intimately with Christ, my friend.... It is the deepest joy the heart can have.[2]

TWELVE

Joy: The Echo of God's Life in Us

Our natural will is to have God, and the good will of God is to have us, and we may never cease willing or longing for him until we have him in the fullness of joy. [Christ] *will never have his full bliss in us until we have our full bliss in him.*

Blessed Julian of Norwich

The saints not only model joy; they tell us from where that joy comes. God alone is the source of that joy that perseveres through life's vicissitudes and brings us to the final eternal bliss.

Blessed Dom Columba Marmion's heart was both jovial and full of spiritual wisdom. Acclaimed as one of the greatest spiritual writers of the twentieth century, his *Christ the Life of the Soul* has become a classic. With a mixture of humility and humor and his usual gentle wit, he commented, "The reason of the success is that there is practically nothing in these works from me."

Born on April Fool's Day in 1858, he often jokingly told people, "I was born a genuine fool." People who had heard of his reputation for holiness and spiritual wisdom were often surprised, on meeting him, to find so jovial a man. His merry temperament was one of his most notable qualities. His joy went far deeper than temperament, however. "Joy is the echo of God's life in us," he wrote.

The years of World War I, with their trials and physical hardships, took their toll on Don Columba's health. As it deteriorated, he found himself experiencing sleepiness at inopportune moments. His sense of humor helped him to deal with this embarrassment.

His sense of humor invariably helped him out of other tight situations. Once he gave Benediction to a group of nuns whose singing was terrible. Afterward their superior asked his opinion of their performance of the chant. He could not lie, but he didn't want to be unkind, so he said, "Look here, my dear sister, there are some who sing so as to imitate the angels and some who sing so as to put demons to flight."

The holy abbot was chosen to lead a group of young monks to Ireland, since not all of them could be supported at the Belgian abbey. He dressed as a civilian to sneak into England without a passport, but he was caught. After all other explanations had failed, he told the inspectors, "I'm Irish, and the Irish never need a passport except for hell, and it isn't there that I am wanting to go." He got across the border.

Joy in Following God

The young Italian Servant of God Carla Ronci was delighted when she realized she could live in union with God.

> The thought that has touched me the most is this: God is in me. I am a living tabernacle. It does not have to be difficult to live in union with God. That means to live an interior life…. I am happy to exist. I am content with everything that surrounds me because in everything I detect a gift from God.[1]

The cheerful young working girl zipped about Rimini on her motor scooter. As a teacher of the youngest and later the teenage members of the Catholic Action youth, Carla arranged outings, parties, amateur theatricals, and other entertainments for her charges. She taught them that love and laughter are perfectly at home in the will of God.

At twenty-four Carla joined the secular institute Handmaids of the Mother of Mercy, whose members remain in the world. Here she was able to have a spiritual life while living with her family. When Carla died in 1969, her confessor was so convinced of her sanctity that he forsook the customary black vestments of the time and celebrated the funeral Mass in white. In his remarks he pointed out the happy truth that sanctity does not lie hidden only in the cloister but can exist in the world, and indeed it is the will of God for it to be so.

Dorothy Day exemplifies the joy of living for God in the world. Toward the end of her life she remained in her room, too ill to go downstairs to receive visitors. There she wrote of her past, her family life, and the early days of the Catholic Worker Movement. One reader of her newspaper, *The Catholic Worker,* wrote to her, "I sense your love of your family in each word you write." Dorothy wrote back, "I hope you sense the joy of my life as well."

If love, even human love, gives so much consolation here, what will love not be in heaven?

Blessed Josemaría Escrivá de Balaguer

Jesus deigned to teach me this mystery. He set before me the book of nature. I understood how all the flowers He has created are beautiful, how the splendor of the rose and the whiteness of the lily do not take away the perfume of the little violet or the delightful simplicity of the daisy. I understood that if all the flowers wanted to be roses, nature would lose her springtime beauty, and the fields would no longer be decked out with little wildflowers.

And so it is in the world of souls, Jesus' garden. He willed to create great souls comparable to lilies and roses, but He has created smaller ones and these must be content to be daisies or violets destined to give joy to God's glances when He looks down at His feet. Perfection consists in doing His will, in being what He wills us to be.[2]

St. Thérèse of Lisieux

God's Indwelling

The priest who prepared her for First Communion told a friend that "with her temperament, Elizabeth Catez will be either a saint or a demon." Through her determination, she conquered her temper so thoroughly that she became known as a gentle and gracious girl who inspired others with peace and joy.

At eighteen Elizabeth spoke to a priest about a mysterious feeling she had of "being dwelt in." He explained that this was true, since the Holy Trinity dwelt in her soul through baptism.

The doctrine of the indwelling of the Trinity in the Christian soul became the core of Blessed Elizabeth of the Trinity's spiritual life. As a cloistered Carmelite, it seemed that no matter what she did, be it pleasant or painful, Elizabeth was very happy. In her writings she outlines the secret of happiness and sanctity hidden in the depths of the soul by the divine indwelling. She once said, "It seems to me that I have found my heaven on earth, for heaven is God and God is in my soul. On the day I understood that, everything became clear to me."

See, this kingdom of God is now found within us. The grace of the Holy Spirit shines forth and warms us, and is overflowing with many and varied scents into the air around us, regales our senses with heavenly delight, as it fills our heart with joy inexpressible.

St. Seraphim of Sarov

The Challenge of Joy

As we have seen, the saints counsel joy. Are we called to seek this joy? The *Catechism* reminds us of the psalmist's words:

> "Let the hearts of those who seek the Lord rejoice." Although man can forget God or reject Him, He never ceases to call every man to seek Him, so as to find life and happiness. But this search for God demands of man every effort of intellect, a sound will, "an upright heart," as well as the witness of others who teach him to seek God.[3]

St. Augustine says, "No one is really happy merely because he has what he wants, but only if he wants things he ought to want." And, "Our heart is restless until it rests in You."

But what of those days when everything is going wrong and we just can't seem to feel that joy? We weren't all born Pollyannas! The saints share with us the hope that this joy will be undeniably ours if we pursue God.

When a man reaches the desirable haven of pure Love, even if he wished and tried his best not to, he can do nothing but love and be joyful.

St. Catherine of Genoa

This joy is contagious. One day at work my friend Karin was disconsolate. Her home had been burglarized, and she was in the process of a divorce. A priest friend happened to call me. Fr. Jim has reminded me on some of my own dark days to look at the world the right way: upside down. I asked him to speak with Karin because she was so upset and sad.

Within a few moments I could hear Karin laughing heartily in the other office. Later she told me that when Father's kind voice came on the line, she spilled out all her unhappiness to him. When she finished, he was silent a brief moment and then told her, "Karin, cheer up. Things could get worse."

He then continued musingly, "You know, one time I had a terrible week and a friend of mine said that to me; he told me to cheer up because things could always get worse. So I cheered up, and sure enough, things did get worse." Karin had to laugh, and her own problems seemed immediately to recede. "Down" days happen. And laughter lifts us.

Help From Heaven

Sometimes the saints are the ones to help us on our "down" days. St. Joseph has bailed our company out of financial difficulties time after time. After one particularly stressful event, when a line of credit was issued by the bank just in time to meet payroll, we elected St. Joseph our "titular vice president in charge of finance." Not knowing his last name, we inscribed him in the corporate minutes as Joseph Nazareno.

One of our corporate officers, a former religion teacher, came to the meeting late. When asked to sign the minutes, she stared at them and then asked, "Who the heck is Joseph Nazareno? Is that the banker Ann has been talking to?"

When Karin and I simultaneously answered, "Oh, yeah!" Heather caught on. The three of us burst into a laughing session that gave us aching sides and happy hearts.

> You must accept your cross; if you carry it courageously, it will carry you to heaven. God commands you to pray, but he forbids you to worry.
>
> *St. John Vianney*

For all of us, being human, melancholy sometimes takes over and clouds our perceptions. Temporarily we just can't seem to see the good, the beauty, the marvelous gifts of our good God. I want to close with the prescriptions three saints give for those days.

> Melancholy is the poison of devotion. When one is in tribulation, it is necessary to be more happy and more joyful because one is nearer to God.
>
> *St. Clare of Assisi*

> Since happiness is nothing other than the enjoyment of the highest good and since the highest good is above, no one can be happy unless he rise above himself, not by an ascent of the body, but of the heart.
>
> *St. Bonaventure*

And the "Angelic Doctor" gives us some very practical advice.

> Sorrow can be alleviated by good sleep, a bath, and a glass of wine.
>
> *St. Thomas Aquinas*

A final toast to you, the reader: May you join merrily in the communion of the saints and follow their wise counsel. May you accept the challenge of joy in your life.

NOTES

Introduction
What Is Joy, and Why Should We Have It?

1. *Catechism of the Catholic Church* (hereafter cited as "CCC"), 1832; Gal 5:22-23 (Vulgate).
2. CCC, 1029; Rv 22:5; see also Mt 15:21, 23.
3. Dorothy Day, *From Union Square to Rome* (Silver Spring, Md.: Preservation of the Faith, 1940), 10.
   Dorothy Day, *The Long Loneliness* (San Francisco: Harper & Row, 1981), 139.

ONE
The Kingdom of Eternal Bliss

1. Aelred of Rievaulx, *A Letter to His Sister*, trans. Geoffrey Webb and Adrian Walker (London: A.R. Mowbray, 1957), 60; quoted in Felicitas Corrigan, O.S.B., *The Saints Humanly Speaking* (Ann Arbor, Mich.: Servant, 2000), 288-89.

TWO
No Sad Saints!

1. St. Augustine, *The Confessions*, IV, 8.
2. Damian Blaher, *The Little Flowers of St. Francis* (New York: E.P. Dutton, 1951), xii.
3. Blessed Pier Giorgio Frassati, letter to his sister, 1925, courtesy of Rev. Bill Kuchinsky.

THREE
Finding Perfect Joy

1. The writings of St. Francis and his early biographers are available in numerous editions and translations; see, for example, *The Writings of St. Francis of Assisi*, Paschal Robinson, trans. (London: O.F.M., 1906); Thomas of Celano, *The Lives of St. Francis of Assisi*, A. G. Ferrers, trans. (London: Howell, 1902); St. Bonaventura, *The Life of St. Francis* (London: Temple Classics, 1904); *Mirror of Perfection*, Robert Steele, trans. (London: Temple Classics, 1903); Brother Ugolino, *The Little Flowers of St. Francis*, Georgina Fullerton, trans. (New York: Heritage, 1910). Quotes in this chapter come from these and similar sources.

FIVE
Laugh at Yourself

1. Quoted in Margaret, Matthew, and Stephen Bunson, *John Paul II's Book of Saints* (Huntington, Ind.: Our Sunday Visitor, 1999), 19.
2. Ferdinand Holbock, *New Saints and Blesseds of the Catholic Church* (San Francisco: Ignatius, 2000), 19.
3. Richard Simpson, *Edmund Campion: A Biography* (London: John Hodges, 1896), 174-76; quoted in Corrigan, 36.
4. Franciscan Friars of the Immaculate, *St. Thérèse, Doctor of the Little Way* (Waite Park, Minn.: Park Press, 1997), 53.

SIX
Enjoy Yourself!

1. Lancelot Sheppard, *Don Bosco* (Westminster, Md: The Newman Press, 1957), 12.
2. Neil Boyton, *The Blessed Friend of Youth* (New York: Macmillan, 1929), 164.
3. Peter Lapin, *Halfway to Heaven* (New Rochelle, N.Y.: Don Bosco Publications, 1981), 159.
4. Lapin, 253.

SEVEN
God Loves a Cheerful Giver

1. Malcolm Muggeridge, *Something Beautiful for God* (New York: Ballantine, 1971), 98.
2. Ann Ball, *Faces of Holiness,* vol. 2 (Huntington, Ind.: Our Sunday Visitor, 2001), 55.
3. Ball, *Faces,* 76.

NINE
Out of the Mouths of Babes

1. Ann Ball, "The Virgin Smiled at Her," *Thirteenth of the Month Club 10* (September 1998), 2.
2. Barbara Gutierrez, *Charlene* (Lafayette, La.: Friends of Charlene, 1988), 24.

TEN
Sometimes It's All Right to Cry

1. Ann Ball, *Blessed Miguel Pro: Twentieth-Century Mexican Martyr* (Rockford, Ill.: TAN, 1996), 33-34.
2. Ann Ball, *Catholic Book of the Dead* (Huntington, Ind.: Our Sunday Visitor, 1995), 100-101. Quote is popularly attributed to St. Augustine.

ELEVEN
The Joy of the Martyrs

1. Ball, *Faces,* 93.
2. Cal Samra, *The Joyful Christ: The Healing Power of Humor* (San Francisco: Harper & Row, 1986), 93, 101.

TWELVE
Joy: The Echo of God's Life in Us

1. Ann Ball, *Faces of Holiness,* vol. 2 (Huntington, Ind.: Our Sunday Visitor, 2001), 33.
2. *Thérèse: A Collection of Meditations* (Reno, Nev.: Carmel of Reno, 1984), 3.
3. CCC, 30; Ps 105:3.

SOURCES

Attwater, Donald. *Saints Westward*. New York: P.J. Kenedy and Sons, 1953.

Ann Ball, *Blessed Miguel Pro: Twentieth-Century Mexican Martyr*. Rockford, Ill.: TAN, 1996.

___. *Catholic Book of the Dead*. Huntington, Ind.: Our Sunday Visitor, 1995.

___. *Faces of Holiness*. Huntington, Ind.: Our Sunday Visitor, 1999.

___. *Faces of Holiness*. Vol. 2. Huntington, Ind.: Our Sunday Visitor, 2001.

___. *Modern Saints, Their Lives and Faces*. Vol. 2. Rockford, Ill.: TAN Books, 1990.

___. "The Virgin Smiled at Her." *Thirteenth of the Month Club* 10 (September, 1998): 2.

Blaher, Damian, ed. *The Little Flowers of St. Francis*. New York: E.P. Dutton and Company, Inc., 1951.

Bunson, Matthew, Margaret, and Stephen. *John Paul II's Book of Saints*. Huntington, Ind.: Our Sunday Visitor, 1999.

Boyton, Neil. *The Blessed Friend of Youth*. New York: Macmillan, 1929.

Chervin, Ronda de Sola. *Quotable Saints*. Ann Arbor, Mich.: Servant, 1992.

Chittister, Joan. *Illuminated Life: Monastic Wisdom for Seekers of Light*. Maryknoll, N.Y.: Orbis, 2000.

Corrigan, Felicitas. *The Saints Humanly Speaking*. Ann Arbor, Mich.: Servant, 2000.

Day, Dorothy. *From Union Square to Rome*. Silver Spring, Md.: Preservation of the Faith, 1940.

Day, Dorothy. *The Long Loneliness*. San Francisco: Harper & Row, 1981.

Franciscan Friars of the Immaculate. *St. Thérèse, Doctor of the Little Way*. Waite Parke, Minn.: Park Press, 1997.

Frassati, Pier Giorgio, Letter to his sister, 1925, courtesy of Rev. Bill Kuchinsky.

Gutierrez, Barbara. *Charlene*. Lafayette, La.: Friends of Charlene, 1988.

Holbock, Ferdinand. *New Saints and Blesseds of the Catholic Church*. San Francisco: Ignatius Press, 2000.

Knowles, Leo. *Saints Who Spoke English*. St. Paul, Minn.: Carillon Books, 1979.

Kondor, Louis. *Fatima in Lucia's Own Words*. Fatima: Postulation Centre, 1976.

Lapin, Peter. *Halfway to Heaven*. New Rochelle, N.Y.: Don Bosco Publications, 1981.

Migne, J.P., ed. *Patrologia Latina*. Paris: 1841-1855.

Muggeridge, Malcolm. *Something Beautiful for God*. New York: Ballantine, 1971.

Norman, Mrs. George. *God's Jester*. New York: Benzinger, 1930.

Samra, Cal. *The Joyful Christ: The Healing Power of Humor*. San Francisco: Harper and Row, 1986.

Sheppard, Lancelot. *Don Bosco*. Westminster, Md.: The Newman Press, 1957.

Thérèse: A Collection of Meditations. Reno, Nev.: Carmel of Reno, 1984.

Tweedie, James. "Joy in a Leper's Colony," *The Joyful Noiseletter* (October 2000) 4.

Vetancurt, Agustin de. *Menologia Franciscano*. J. Michael Walker, trans. Mexico City, 1698.

Several quotes and anecdotes in this volume come from an especially helpful source, *The Joyful Noiseletter,* edited by Cal Samra. Cal knows the healing power of humor. Barely twenty years ago, he was in the depths of depression and despair. He determined to end it all, bought some sturdy rope, and drove all over the Phoenix, Arizona area hunting for a tree from which to hang himself. The palm trees were too tall to climb, so he finally found a very tall cactus in the desert, where he sat for some time contemplating how to hang himself from it.

Some hours later, Cal found himself in a chapel, pouring out his pain, praying for the strength to endure and go on. He did go on to find the healing power of humor, which he explains in his book *The Joyful Christ* (see above). In 1985, he and his wife, Rose, began the Fellowship of Merry Christians, an ecumenical group with the modest aim of recapturing the spirit of joy, humor, and unity, and the healing power of the early Christians.

The Fellowship's membership includes thousands of Catholic and Protestant pastors, as well as lay people of all persuasions. Their monthly newsletter, *The Joyful Noiseletter,* provides pastors, laypeople, and church newsletter editors with holy humor, joyful Scriptural references, and cartoons that can be used in sermons or reprinted in church newsletters. Interested readers should write The Fellowship of Merry Christians, P.O. Box 895, Portage, MI 49081-0895; online, go to www.JOYFULNOISELETTER.com or call toll-free 1-800-877-2757.

INDEX